To Danielle,
Merry Christmas 202
From Paul
P.D.J. 06/12

C000050368

# The Data Garden
*And Other Datallegories*

*The World's First Book of Data Allegories:*
*6 Lessons In Effective Data Management*

PAUL DANIEL JONES

The stories in this book are fictional. Names, characters, places and incidents are either the product of the author's imagination or are used fictitiously. Any resemblance to actual persons, living or dead, events, or locales, is entirely coincidental.

Copyright © 2020 Paul Daniel Jones

http://www.pauldanieljones.com


All rights reserved. No part of this book may be reproduced or used in any manner without written permission of the copyright owner except for the use of quotations in a book review.

First paperback edition September 2020


ISBN: 979-8-68444-032-8

EDP   Expert
      Data
      Publication

# DEDICATION

*For Tristan, Elysia and Ethan*

# PRAISE FOR THE DATA GARDEN

**"It was a joy to read"**

*Simone Steel, Chief Data Officer, Nationwide Building Society*

**"Great read, fun but so many lessons - as I finished I wanted to read it again - bravo!!"**

*Gareth Davies, Executive Vice President – Risk Management, Wells Fargo*

**"Paul's data stories are a fantastic way to introduce these topics to non-data experts. I'll be using them as part of engaging with my business colleagues on our data literacy change programme."**

*Rob McKendrick, Head of Data, The Co-Op*

**"Paul has a rare gift for explaining the complexities of data management in a simple manner, without being simplistic. His collection of allegories bring the subject to life for battle-weary experts and newbies alike. This fantastic little book will help you cultivate a thriving data culture, without leading you down the garden path."**

*David Blackwell, Lead Partner for Data, Analytics and AI - Baringa Partners*

"This easy to read set of stories is a really helpful tool for management and executives, who know Data is an asset to their organisation, but don't really understand why or how to harness greater value from it. It's a significant help to cut through the Data mumbo jumbo that acts as a barrier to progress in most organisations"

*Nigel Walder, COO, ClearBank*

"The Data Garden brings to life the challenges of managing and utilising data in an organisation for a non-technical audience through a series of allegories and stories that everyone can understand and in doing so sheds light on practical steps that every organisation should take to get on top of their data. Entertaining and thought provoking, the stories will help experienced data specialists communicate why data governance and management needs to be handled strategically to develop insight and data driven decision making."

*Simon Williams, CEO, NTT Data UK*

"Unique and powerful storytelling to lay emphasis on data literacy, governance and value realisation - wonderful read indeed"

*Rodney Coutinho, Senior Director (AI, Digitalisation & Data), Publicis Sapient*

# CONTENTS

# INTRODUCTION: THE DATALLEGORIES

**"Purposeful storytelling isn't show business, it's good business."**
*Peter Guber, CEO of Mandalay Entertainment*

**Prepare to experience a new way of thinking about Data Management.**

The world's top businesses depend on data to drive their success. Every digital transformation runs on data, and the best customer experiences are delivered through the intelligent use of data.

The fact is, effective data management is not just important to build competitive advantage, it's also absolutely essential to survive and thrive in the modern business world.

Over the past few decades, Data Management has made the transition from being an evolving collection of practices, which a handful of organisations attempted to apply to get ahead, to being a well-established profession, which is widely acknowledged as a necessity for the modern enterprise.

In addition to the clear commercial value of managing data properly, there are also an increasing number of laws and regulations that are forcing companies to make data management a Board-level priority. As a result, senior executives need to understand enough to be able to be effective in their roles as sponsors of these important initiatives.

There are many good books and articles published about the subject, mostly in classic business textbook fashion, and some of which are very informative. The trouble is, unless you're a data professional, the nuts and bolts of "how to do it" can all be a bit... well... *dry*.

1

Not only that, but successful data management initiatives involve a very wide range of disciplines and techniques, which, due to the apparent scale of the undertaking, can make them difficult for people to get their heads around.

So what can we do about it?

I give you this book of Data Management Allegories (or "Datallegories"). Instead of yet another textbook of data management theory, the stories in this book offer a set of metaphors, analogies and allegories that explain key data management concepts using familiar scenarios that should make it easier for non-technical and non-data-geeky people to understand.

In this book, you are invited to explore worlds, both familiar and fantastic, which will tap into your imagination and illuminate a range of topics that are vitally important to data management, yet so often misunderstood and over-complicated with jargon and techno-babble, masking their underlying simplicity.

The stories have been carefully crafted to weave several rich layers of experiences and lessons into them, gathered through many years of data management practice.

If you are a senior executive and recognise the importance of data but need a better understanding to be able to play an effective role as sponsor to a data management initiative, these simple stories will provide a high-level introduction to key topics, using real-world imagery and scenarios that should be easy to visualise and understand, without the data jargon.

For the data management professional, there are a range of lessons that you'll find built into these analogies, which are helpful to remember when you're running your own initiative, and may help you when you need to explain things to non-technical audiences. Whilst the allegories are each written to be understood by a data management novice, there's a lot more in every one of them than initially meets the eye, including the odd in-joke that only a seasoned data expert will spot!

Whatever you are aiming to get out of this book, I hope you find these allegories fun to read, thought provoking and insightful in equal measure.

Now, let's start with a spot of data gardening, shall we…?

# 1. THE DATA GARDEN

## Welcome to the Data Garden

In this little Data Garden, the plants and trees are data. They've all been planted for a purpose. Some are there to bear fruit. Others are there to look beautiful and provide the users of the garden with joy. Some are there to combine with other plants; and there is a single tree, which was planted to fix a swing to, for children to play on.

The garden is on a particular plot of south-facing land, which has been cultivated for its owners to derive value and satisfaction from. The owners often go for strolls in the garden, and also provide access to it and its abundant resources for others to enjoy. They charge a small price for admission, so they are able to profit from sharing its many benefits with others.

Everything in the garden grows over time. The grass grows deep and long; the bushes expand into thick hedgerows; and the flowers bloom and blossom in all manner of colours, as they spread throughout the landscape.

All of this growth is good and fruitful; but over time, it can also become unwieldy. As the garden becomes overgrown, it becomes cluttered and harder to access. Wiry branches stretch into open spaces; weeds establish a foothold and risk choking the plants that were so carefully placed; and everything starts becoming so overwhelmingly messy.

Also, as the garden gets used, some of the plants and landscape become damaged. Data flowers are trampled so their shape and colours are lost; the patch of grass under the swing becomes an unsightly, scuffed mud patch; and patches appear across the lawn, noticeable gaps across the once lush green carpet.

The owners realise that something must be done. They cannot enjoy their little data garden as they once did, and their profits are being affected too. They make up their mind: they must appoint a gardener.

Congratulations! You've been appointed to be the *Data Gardener*!


## Mowing the Data Lawn

The Data Lawn is used by families to play on, so it must be kept in good condition and must not become overgrown. However, like all data, the data grass grows every day, as do all of the other plants and shrubs throughout the garden.

As a result of all this growth, the lawn must be mowed at least once every two weeks; and sometimes once a week, during the summer months. Of course, exactly how fast the lawn grows depends on all kinds of factors, such as how much sun it is exposed to and how well it is watered. Also, it can be damaged through mis-use, which can result in the need for patches of spoilt or missing grass to be repaired or replaced.

One thing is for certain though: it's a never-ending job. No matter what you do, you can't stop the grass from growing; and if you want people to be able to get the most out of it and for the garden's owners to profit from it, you've got to look after it.

Given the size of the garden, it's not that big a task to maintain it by yourself and you've been able to quite comfortably keep on top of it, with your small, manual lawnmower and a few basic gardening tools.

You've established a little routine for yourself, regularly reviewing the state of the garden and its plants, and taking action to tend to them based on how well they're getting on. Different data plants grow and age differently; some are more susceptible to damage when people use the garden than others; and as such, the frequency with which you check on them and the things you do to keep them in healthy condition vary. The good thing is, because you know what each of the plants are and the best way to treat them, you can make sure you treat them in the right way, at the right time. Plus, because you keep checking them at regular intervals, if anything unexpected happens, like unanticipated damage from a particularly heavy-footed user of the garden, you can do something about it straight away.

You're paid a fair hourly rate for your work, and the owners are happy with the service you provide. So happy in fact, that they decide to offer you some more work…

Congratulations! You've been appointed to be the *Head Data Landscape Gardener*!

## The Data Landscape Garden

As well as the small garden that you've been looking after by yourself, you've now been entrusted with a modest-sized landscape garden to tend to.

This garden is far more sophisticated and is used for a wider range of activities. It has a path that winds its way from the entrance around the perimeter, passing through a small wooded area to a sheltered pavilion, next to an open area that has been laid to grass and is used for various medium-sized events such as weddings and family gatherings.

Given the size and complexity of the garden, the owners had already employed two part-time gardeners, who they have now put under your charge. They also know that you'll need to take a different approach to its maintenance, so offer you a budget and ask you to come back with some ideas on how to improve the way that the data landscape garden is maintained.

Having learnt from the first garden, you start by taking some time to understand the garden. You talk to your new colleagues to understand what they know about the garden, what's working and what isn't. You create an inventory of the plants and shrubs and trees; and examine their condition, noting areas that require particular care.

Initially, while you're building an understanding of the garden, you allow the incumbent part-time gardeners to continue to operate in the way that they had been before, and only make a few minor tweaks to their routines, based on some things that you could immediately see could be improved, and based on your experience.

However, once you have developed your inventory of plants and their condition, you can start to implement some improvements, to make the garden more productive and to be more efficient in the way in which it is looked after.

There are data flowerbeds that line some of the pathways around the garden, which need regular watering to keep the data flowers healthy. Currently, the part-time gardeners need to regularly check the condition of the flowers to determine whether they need watering, then use heavy watering cans, which they fill up at a tap near the garden entrance and carry across to the data flowers. Each time, this can involve multiple trips from the tap and it's a tiring and time-consuming exercise. It also means that the gardeners, who have expertise in the care of some of the more rare and valuable plants in other parts of the garden, spend a disproportionate amount of time carrying water backwards and forwards, when their time could be utilised in far more valuable activities.

So, the first investment that you make is in an automatic sprinkler system. The system is designed to provide the optimum amount of water to the data flowerbeds and totally removes the need for any gardeners to spend their time watering them. This frees them up to focus on the parts of the garden where they can cultivate the more interesting and exotic plants, which are more fruitful, more pleasing to the owners and will attract more paying visitors.

The next part of the garden that you turn your attention to, is the open space that is used for events. As you stand at the highest part of the garden and the gentle, warm summer breeze ruffles the long grass, your experienced eyes note the size and shape of the area as you quietly calculate the scale of effort it would take to mow and maintain it. You smile as you think of your little, manual lawnmower and how great it's been for the small Data Garden; yet how totally inadequate it would be for this new challenge.

The next day, you return with a new, ride-on lawnmower. It was quite costly, but you know that by keeping the open space well groomed, it will be far easier to utilise and obtain value from; plus, it will be easier for prospective users to see how they could use it, so you know you'll be able to encourage more people to hold their weddings and corporate events here, delivering income that far exceeds the cost of the lawnmower. Plus, of course, using a shiny new ride-on lawnmower is far easier, faster and more fun than using the old manual mower; and it means that the other part-time gardeners are keen to help out too!

Your efforts are paying off. Visitor numbers are higher than ever and the owners are delighted with your work. However, with high levels of usage, you start to encounter different problems...

## Dealing with Data Litter

The first problem is one that you're already used to from the smaller data garden: wear and tear. As such, because you and your part-time data gardener colleagues understand the plants and what needs to be done to care for them, you can quickly establish a routine for this. Together, you pro-actively replace patches of grass, cordon off and re-seed where needed, re-plant flowers, and implement a range of other measures. The key difference in this larger garden turns out to be the way in which you monitor the plants: it's too big to check all plants every day, and there's no more budget for additional technology or more people, so you have to put in place a prioritised, manual system of checking different plants at different intervals, depending on the likelihood that they will be damaged and also, in some cases, based on their value.

One thing that you also do, which is different from the smaller data garden and turns out to be quite effective, is to ask users of the data landscape garden to report damage to you and your colleagues. Whilst many users don't report anything, there are some who do, and this additional feed of intelligence helps quickly catch some problems before the plants are irreparably damaged.

However, the biggest problem that comes with all of the new visitors, which is a new one to you, is the Data Litter.

It turns out that some data users are very careless and messy. They drop their rubbish as they walk along the pathways and it gets caught up in the flowerbeds and significantly detracts from the beauty of the landscape. In some cases, it also causes harm to the plants and wildlife, which is an even greater concern.

Initially, you and your data gardener colleagues attempt to tidy the place yourselves, but data litter picking quickly becomes a full-time job in itself!

You need to try a different approach.

In order to work out what to do, you contact an experienced gardener friend of yours to understand what she does for one of the many, much larger gardens that she manages. Her insights are invaluable. She takes the time to show you some of the systems and ideas that she's tried over time, including what's worked well and what hasn't. You can't thank her enough – it gives you all the ideas you need to turn things around.

Now, when you return to your landscape garden, you know exactly what you're going to do; and the biggest shift in thinking is to start to actively engage with your data users. They are the ones who gain the most value from the garden being in a good and well-maintained state; and they are also the ones who are now having the greatest impact on the data garden's health. Before you do anything, you talk to the owners to explain your ideas and obtain their support. They recognise the challenges you're facing and trust you based on the good work you've done for them to date, so agree to your ideas and say that you can call on them if you need anything. With a feeling of hope, you get to work.

The first thing you do is to install bins throughout the site. They are positioned as discreetly as possible, but in places where you know the most litter is dropped. You make it as easy for the users to access and use them as possible, because you understand that it is important to make things easy for people if you want them to do something new. You also agree a routine of litter bin collection with your data gardener colleagues, so you'll be able to both monitor their use and to keep them from overflowing.

Next, you put signs up at the entrance to the data garden and throughout the site, to provide clear guidance on how to get the most out of using the garden, including its rules. However, you make a point to emphasise the points about getting the most out of the garden and the benefits of your guidance, so you don't just make the signs about rules. This was one of the things you saw worked well at your friend's data gardens and you're keen to replicate this approach.

Finally, and most importantly, you change the way that people are welcomed into the data garden. You make sure that each visitor, when they pay for access, is met with a friendly introductory chat. This up-front engagement is used to understand how they will be using the garden so they can be provided with tailored tips on getting the best out of the data based on what they are trying to do, and also so that the rules of the data garden are clearly explained and agreed to before they enter.

## Choosing proportionate measures

The new measures you've put in place to deal with the data litter are a great success. Even better, the increased engagement with data users leads to better relationships with them and improved use and maintenance of the data garden as a whole.

However, there were some additional things you could have done, which you consciously chose not to, because you knew that they were too heavy-handed for this particular data garden. In the very biggest garden estates that your data gardener friend looked after, she had implemented CCTV monitoring for the areas where it was required and even security guards to enforce the rules.

For the biggest data gardens, these kinds of measures were clearly necessary, especially in situations where there were valuables that need to be protected or where there were dangers, whereby breaking the rules could put data users at serious risk. However, these stronger measures bring with them increased costs and detrimental impacts on the experience for data users, such as privacy concerns, which need to be carefully considered in a balanced way before implementing them.

Given that the data landscape garden that you're looking after doesn't have any really high value contents that could be stolen and doesn't have any serious dangers, you knew that trying some of the less heavy-handed measures and seeing if they work was the sensible first step. If they hadn't worked, you could have considered other measures, but after monitoring the effects of the actions that you tried first, you knew that there was no need to do any more.

Your owners are delighted with the way in which you've handled their two gardens. You've put in place systems that are proportionate for their size and complexities, which have enabled you to maintain and develop them so that they have become more fruitful and delivered far more use and value than they did before.

One late afternoon, after the gates to the data landscape garden have closed, you are sat out with the owners, enjoying the sights and sounds of nature surrounding you. You discuss the journey that you've been on together, from the early days working on the small data garden, to the challenges tackled and overcome in this, now wonderful, data landscape garden.

The discussion soon moves to the future.

The data garden owners are planning on expanding their operation by acquiring a number of large garden estates, at far greater scale than anything they've done before; and they'd like you to be a part of their enterprise.

This next venture would be totally different from before, because it would be far too big for you as a data gardener to be hands-on in the running of each of the gardens. You would need to build a team of experienced gardeners to run each of the gardens and would need to establish management structures and systems to optimise the value that all of these various gardens could deliver overall.

This greater scale and scope could open up fantastic new opportunities to share resources across gardens, to develop totally new events and ways to generate value from the gardens. There could be opportunities and options possibly not yet imagined…

Congratulations! You've been appointed to be the *Chief Data Gardening Officer*.

---

**Lesson 1:**

*Data Management is like gardening. It's a never-ending task, because data keeps growing in volume and variety; but with the right expertise and leadership, and by utilising the right techniques and tools, you can keep your data well maintained, and cultivate it to deliver outstanding value.*

---

# 2. THE DATA GOVERNANCE COUNTRY

## Your Data Governance Country needs you!

In this Data Country, the people are data. The data people each have their own individual characteristics: some are highly skilled and work in productive jobs that contribute to the economy and society; others may be less qualified but perform tasks that are totally essential to the running of the country; some are entrepreneurs that take steps to innovate and generate new value through business. There are also some who are less useful and make fewer contributions to the Data Governance Country. Worse, there are a small minority of data people who are corrupt and dishonest; who appear to be one thing but are something entirely different and drive chaos, disruption and misery for the wider population. Usually these sorry data souls exist because they've been neglected and lost touch with their reason for existing.

The country is vast and rapidly growing, with a population of over a billion data people and counting. The faster the population grows, the more economic and social value can be generated; but at the same time, the spread of resources to look after the data people and get the best out of them diminishes, resulting in an ever greater chance for corruption and poverty.

When the Data Governance Country was young, it was so much easier for the data people to get along and to be productive and happy together. They were so few in numbers, it made collaboration simple, and it was easy to spot the bad apples and deal with them quickly, so that corruption was stamped out before it could take root. Everyone knew each other, everyone knew what role each data person played in their little society and everyone could coordinate their efforts and play their part in a happy, healthy data environment.

Now that the data country is so big, it's not so easy to keep a handle on things. There is a lack of order, a lack of efficiency, and as a result, many data people are suffering and are unable to play their most productive role for the country.

Just like any country, a government has been established to run things and to help the data people to live better, happier, more productive lives.

You are the Head of the new Data Government, and you have quite a task ahead of you…

## The Winning Data Governance Manifesto

You are the Leader of the Data Excellence Party, which has just been appointed as the new government of the Data Country, based on the promises that were made for a better future. When you took over as leader for the party, before you started campaigning, you worked with your leadership team to develop a manifesto that outlined the policies that would be proposed to address the priorities of the data people.

In recent years, economic output has dropped, crime is up, health issues are rising, the population is aging but less productive; and businesses are struggling to innovate and grow. Urgent change is needed.

In order to develop a manifesto that really resonated with the data population and clearly talked to their passions and priorities, you directed the Data Excellence Party to conduct a range of surveys and public engagement exercises to get to the bottom of the issues that are affecting people. Based on this research, a manifesto could be compiled to incorporate a set of policies and budgets, which are all aimed at tackling the issues that data people were talking about, including:
- Police and criminal justice system;
- Healthcare and wellbeing;
- Pensions and funerals;
- Education and research;
- Transport and infrastructure;
- Business and innovation.

The manifesto was revolutionary and led to a landslide victory. It was really clear in the way it explained how each policy would meet widely accepted problems in a practical way.

The other thing that really built credibility with data voters throughout the campaign, was the way your party acknowledged that it would be through the coordinated implementation of all of these policies, not any one individual solution in isolation, which would be the key to delivering transformational improvements across the data country. Everyone knows that doing one thing on its own won't work: success will depend on a well-orchestrated combination of improvements.

Your party also made it clear that success would depend on the willing participation and active engagement of data people across the country. No single one of these initiatives would work on their own, and none of them would work without data people's involvement... but together, with faith and determination, there is a glimmer of hope that this could be the chance that the data country has been waiting for: a chance of a better future and renewed prosperity for all.

## Government, Not Management

It's an amazing victory to win power, but you know that you and your party have signed up to a massive challenge and expectations are high. You also know that you're going to need to make full use of the powers that the Data Government has to influence large-scale change. In order to do this, it's important to know how Data Governance works.

For starters, you know that a Data Government "governs" its data people, it doesn't "manage" them.

Each data person has their own data life, being born into a data family and performing various tasks and activities throughout their lives until their purpose is fulfilled and they expire. Most of these data people don't work for the government, they have their own jobs and businesses and other enterprises. As such, most data people can't be treated like employees or civil servants: they need to be allowed to have a sufficient level of freedom to be able to fulfil their duties, keep healthy and live happy, productive lives.

So, before you get started, let's review what your Data Government is able to do, so you can develop a strategy for implementing your party's manifesto.

In simple terms, the tasks that your government can perform, can be summarised as the following four key things:

1. Set policies, laws and targets;
2. Communicate them;
3. Report on the fulfilment of them;
4. Enforce them.

Let's take a simple example to illustrate this.

The roads of your Data Country are heavily congested, which is making it difficult for people to get to work and causes massive frustration amongst the data population.

So, you could set a new policy about congestion levels and pass a law about variable speed limits on key roads, with a target to decrease congestion during peak hours by 20% and increase the satisfaction of data people in their journeys by 10%. These are your new policies, laws and targets.

Once you've set the new laws, you need to communicate them. The communications need to go out to different audiences in different ways: your data police force need to understand the new laws and how they need to enforce them, so they can be issued formal communications via official channels; the data public need to know what they need to do differently, so they can be engaged via a combination of letters and other media such as TV, radio and adverts on the web; and civil servants working for your data government need to know how they will engage with the public on these new laws and how they will monitor them, so could be provided with briefings through a communications cascade down the government chain of command.

Following the communication of the new rules, it's important to monitor their fulfilment, in relation to the targets that have been set. You'll need baseline data from before the publication of the rules, to be able to monitor changes from then to now. Then you can look at differences over time, to see if your policies are having the desired effect or not. You need to have a clearly defined way of measuring these things both initially and on an ongoing basis, to be able to do this reliably and meaningfully.

Finally, you need to enforce the new rules. How you do so will depend on the type of rule and how important and urgent it is. Will breaking the rules lead to a fine? Or will they lead to a removal of the rights of data people to work until they've resolved the problem that they've caused by breaking the rules? Or will you follow a more positive approach, rewarding people to following the rules rather than punishing non-compliance? You need to work out how you'll make sure your rules are adopted and policed, to be able to roll them out effectively.

All of the above need careful consideration and planning before they're implemented, to ensure they deliver the best possible outcomes. You need to consider questions such as: how will the communication, monitoring and enforcement happen? When you roll the changes out, will you follow a "carrot" approach and sell the benefits so people want to comply, or a "stick" approach and warn about the sanctions associated with non-compliance? Will you need more civil servants to be able to track the data and more police to enforce the new rules? Will all of this work be coordinated centrally, or via local data councils? How will the changes be funded? Will there be central funding made available to support local implementation, or will data people be expected to pick up the costs themselves?

There are quite a number of factors to think about, and this will be the case for each and every policy you decide to implement.

This basic structure of setting rules, communicating them, tracking compliance and enforcing them, is the same pattern that is followed for most aspects of government. The extent to which it's done centrally or locally, how closely it's tracked and how firmly the rules are enforced may all vary, depending on the types of data people affected and the types of rules; but this framework can be used to drive large-scale improvements across a large data population.

OK, now you're clear on this, time to apply the framework to the policies in your manifesto...

## Missing data people, data crime and data corruption

Your first priority is addressing Data Crime. The data people that participated in your party's surveys unanimously agreed that this was the number one problem. Corruption is rife and spreading, and innocent data people are going missing or being injured as they're affected by, or caught in the crossfire of, various criminal activities. Data people are becoming fearful and are less confident going out and doing their jobs. There are stories of good data people doing their best to do the right thing but delivering damagingly poor results because they've been corrupted without even realising it.

Before tackling enforcement of the law, you need to straighten out the law itself. The Data Country's legal system has evolved over many years and has become confused and inconsistent. There are now crimes taking place, for which no laws have ever been developed, so in some cases it's no wonder there is so much discontent amongst the data population. It makes it hard for data people to understand and equally difficult for the data police to interpret and enforce.

As the leader of the Data Excellence Party, you can use the mandate obtained through the recent landslide election, to introduce sweeping reforms. You propose a new, simplified structure for the written laws, starting with high level, easy to understand definitions, then drilling down into detailed technical definitions that can be used to implement them in practice. You place a particular emphasis on helping missing data people, given how widespread a problem it is, before dealing with other more specialist types of data corruption.

The new laws receive a mixed response. Some data people criticise the increased level of scrutiny that they'll be placed under and complain about the impact on their rights and freedoms. Others welcome the changes, praising the clarity and focus on helping those in need.

Whether the updated laws will have the desired impact or not will depend on the way that they are rolled out and upheld. Under your direction, the Data Government instigates a large-scale, multi-media communications campaign, explaining the new rules that people need to follow, with a strong emphasis on the benefits to them and their lives. Data people will be safer. Data corruption will come down. Everyone will be able to fulfil their purpose in life more confidently.

Next, you need to work out how these new rules will be enforced. Various local police forces have existed for some time, but they're scattered across the land and inconsistent in the way they operate and their effectiveness. Some, mainly in the more affluent areas, are well funded and have plenty of data police officers to uphold the peace. Others have been neglected and have staff that are untrained, so don't even really know what they're supposed to be doing.

In order to coordinate a cross-Country set of improvements, you establish a new, central Strategic Data Police team, with authority over all localised data police forces. Some of the more established and effective data police forces are initially sceptical and resistant to this idea, but they are given an opportunity to become leading members of a wider police community, sharing their best practices and working together to drive improvements at a scale that they could never have achieved on their own, which seems to dramatically improve the levels of uptake and support for this new way of working.

To ensure there is a workforce to match the new levels of work, investments are made into new staff, additional training, and new ways of monitoring crime consistently across all parts of the Data Country. For the first time, you will be able to accurately communicate crime levels and use this to both show improvements and to derive insights that will enable targeted investigation and enforcement operations, where they're most needed.

The Data Country's turnaround has started. You know it's only the beginning: crime will always exist and your legal system will always need to adapt and evolve with changes in data markets, technologies and culture, which will all drive changes in the data population and its behaviour. The difference is, you now have the foundations in place. The laws are clear. You have a way of monitoring and enforcing them, which you can adjust based on fluctuations in different crime levels and based on the impact that your interventions are having.

While this has all been progressing, your government has also been working on the data people's second priority...

**Data health crisis: is prevention better than a cure?**

Public health levels have been deteriorating over many years and the problems seem to be accelerating towards a crisis. Data diseases are spreading; data quality health issues are widespread and worsening; and this is all leading to inactivity, which is further impacting data people's health.

Data people need to be well in order to be productive. If they're not productive, it impacts the economy and leads to a range of other unexpected knock-on impacts. Unemployment levels increase, leading to poverty and increased costs for the government. Also, the health service in the Data Country is largely funded by the government, so the more people that are sick, the more budget needs to be put aside to support it.

The first thing most people think about when talking about healthcare is the hospitals and specialist care for injuries and serious diseases. However, one thing that came across clearly in your party's engagement with the public, was that local engagement is an area that's currently really weak.

You know that pouring money into the hospitals will only increase capacity to deal with symptoms once they've got so bad they need higher levels of care. It won't address the wider public health emergency that is clearly developing across the country.

In order to develop a strategy, you bring together top experts from across the country, with knowledge of the challenges faced in each area and the key health problems that are causing the most issues. To your surprise, a lot of the issues are to do with bad habits that data people have adopted in their day-to-day lives. If they behaved differently and stopped being so lazy in the way that they do their jobs and keep their data homes tidy, there would be a dramatic improvement in data health, resulting in a decreased need for use of hospital and other emergency health services.

In response to this expert advice, a public health campaign is launched to explain the benefits of healthier living and to encourage data people to behave in better ways, to decrease the likelihood of them becoming injured or sick. Also, new laws are drafted to place responsibilities on employers to ensure their data employees are kept safe and encouraged to behave appropriately at work.

In addition to these measures, data doctors in local communities are provided with more funding to enable them to support the implementation of the new public health guidance and reduce the burden on the big hospitals and more centralised services.

Central health services have received the lion's share of funding and support over previous years. The hope is that through the implementation of new, more localised data health strategy, that the strain on these central services will reduce. However, for now, they are still needed more than ever and the key enhancement made to their role is to play a stronger part in coordinating the efforts across local authorities and collating information on the impact of these efforts, so that they can be tracked at an aggregate level across the Country and decisions can be made on the prioritisation of efforts and resources.

It doesn't take long for this new approach to have an effect. The simple act of educating the public on how to look after their own data health almost immediately results in an improvement in the quality of many data people's lives. Hospital admissions are starting to fall and public opinion of the Data Excellence party is strengthening by the day.

The next priority is a bit of a controversial one. It's linked to health, but something about health that is a bit of a unique issue for data people...

## Dealing with the Living Dead

Unlike organic lifeforms, data people can live for a very long time and even once they've died, their bodies don't waste away to nothing. They continue to exist, in the exact state that they were, until action is taken to deal with them. An even more unusual thing about deceased data people, is that sometimes they can be mistaken for living data and can be brought back to be used for the purpose that they existed for when they were alive, resulting in all kinds of unintended consequences. Data ghosts don't mean to be disruptive, but unless their metadata status has been changed once they've passed away, they don't have any way of knowing they're dead themselves, so just dutifully do whatever it is they think they should do, which can lead to very unfortunate outcomes for the data businesses that are employing them.

Data zombies still incur costs, and the money's got to come from somewhere. Often, they are left lying alone in their data homes, which still need their bills paying, even if the data people don't need the heating or electricity anymore.

The thing is, moving deceased data people to data archive morgues or to data deletion crematoriums, costs money in itself, and no-one wants to pay it, even though the cost of keeping them where they are very quickly increases to a point where it exceeds the cost of dealing with them properly and humanely in the first place.

The central government has a massive pension fund set aside, which is used to cover the ongoing cost of data people who aren't productive any more but need to be supported in their old homes. This is clearly a cost that needs to be addressed, not least to avoid the increasing number of reported data poltergeists, terrorising workplaces and causing all kinds of mayhem.

In order to address this, as with all other aspects of government, the first step is to develop some rules, which can be communicated and enforced. Under the new rules, all data people, throughout their lives, must regularly report their metadata life status to the government, based on a set of new, published criteria.

Once a data person has passed to a point where they are no longer actively working, they must be assessed to determine whether they are ever likely to be needed in the future, of if they have truly expired and are no longer living, breathing data with a purpose. Depending on this assessment, the data person will either be moved to a data archive retirement home, which is based outside of the towns and cities and is generally far cheaper than needing to cover the full costs of their active data residence; or they will be sent to be humanely dealt with at a data deletion crematorium.

Some businesses are worried about this. The most common concern that you hear is: "What if we need the data people again at some point in the future?" This is where the assessment criteria become important: there's no problem with data people being sustained in whatever data archive residence is appropriate for them, if there's a good reason to do so, and this could mean many years after their active duties have been completed. However, the new rules state that it is not permissible to sustain data people indefinitely, unless they are likely to be actively used again in the future. Different types of data people may need to be kept in a condition that would enable them to work for longer than others, but only with a clear purpose. Otherwise, there's no excuse for incurring the ongoing costs and it's unfair on the data people themselves, who deserve to rest in peace!

The new policies related to reducing the dependency on state pensions and increasing the number of funerals is initially controversial and resisted. However, you decide to shift the cost of ongoing maintenance to local Data Councils rather than the central government. This is initially even more unpopular, but quickly drives a very different set of behaviours. When the cost lands with the local councils, they start seeking opportunities to reduce the amount of time data people are sustained for, beyond their active working lives, which leads to an increase in data people being archived and cremated.

No matter what people's views are on these new policies, there is no doubt that the reduction in inactive data people frees up money and resources to spend on other, more important areas requiring investment. There's also a decrease in the mis-use of deceased data people, resulting in far fewer negative outcomes for companies.

When you have time, you might sit back and reflect on this. Sometimes, just because a policy is unpopular, doesn't mean it's the wrong thing to do. In this case, holding your nerve against the negative public opinion, is resulting in positive outcomes for the country; and as the results of these changes start to shine through, it won't be long before public opinion shifts in your favour again.

In the meantime, you need to make sure you're making progress on your next policy...

# Developing data people for the future

Now you've made progress on the "defensive" policies, which protect your data population from harm and reduce corruption and injury, you can start to move to policies that will drive real value.

Data people are only valuable when they're put to work; and the more sophisticated the work they're used for, the more value they can drive. The more value they drive, the more money they make and the better it is for your Data Country's economy.

The thing is, as with all people, data people need to be educated to build the skills they need to drive value. Without good education, they'll just sit there with a lot of latent value but won't actually do anything.

Fortunately, there is a basic education system that's already in place for your Data Country, so you have something to build on. However, the subjects that are taught are mostly very superficial and aren't empowering the data workforce with knowledge and skills that will enable them to compete with data people in other countries.

Your party initiates a new education programme, which sets a curriculum and target grades for schools and education service providers. This programme covers:
- Basic data literacy, for all data people;
- Education on how to ensure new things are built to maximise value, for data people such as architects and infrastructure engineers;
- Education on how to manage data people to get the most out of them, for business owners and data people managers;
- Research, development and education on advanced new ways to deliver more value through data people.

The idea behind structuring the education programme this way, is to target different audiences with relevant messages, which will increase their understanding and drive improvements to their productivity and the value they deliver for themselves and the economy.

Now you run into a problem... your budget is starting to look very stretched. The trouble is, you know that getting education right is absolutely fundamental to making your Data Country more productive and more competitive. You've got to be able to do something about it, but you also still need enough money to support the delivery of your other policies. Also, education is one of those things that doesn't pay off immediately, which means some are reluctant to invest in it: it will take time to upskill data people and start seeing the benefits; but the longer you delay investment in it, the longer it will take to see the payoff, so it's best to start early, even if you have to start small.

After a discussion with the minister in charge of the data government's treasury, you agree a way forward. The basic data literacy will be fully funded by the government. That will mean that the broadest population of people will be provided with basic data skills, which will improve their ability to deliver value and also provide the foundations for them to build their skills and expertise further.

When it comes to targeted education for data people who build new things, and for data people managers, these topics will form part of the mandatory curriculum for data literacy, but there's limited funding available beyond this, so further education will receive some minimal subsidisation. You'd like to be able to do more, and in future years, once the other policies have really made some traction, maybe you'll be able to, but this is all you can afford at this time.

Finally, the higher education institutions will be encouraged to seek private funding for research and for more advanced courses, plus you'll also look into options for further funding for this, as part of the "business and innovation" policy, so there should still be some opportunities to invest and stimulate opportunities in the future.


**Data people need to be able to travel**

By the time you get to your transport and infrastructure policy, your budget is nearly spent. You've rightly prioritised the policies that will help directly improve your data population's standard of living and set them up for healthier, happier, safer and more productive lives, but when you get to the stage where everyone is well educated, how are they going to get to the new jobs where they're going to be able to deliver this enhanced value?

The more valuable data people become, the higher the demand for their services, and the more they need to travel to be used in different places. In fact, in many cases, data people can't do any work at all until they've travelled somewhere, so transport is absolutely critical.

Fortunately, your Minister for Transport and Infrastructure has an idea. Whereas most of your other policies depend on central government funding, raised through taxes, the new idea is to develop proposals for a series of strategic infrastructure projects and to invite businesses to invest in them.

For this first year, to get things started, the proposal that you'll ask companies to bid for, will be for a new business development on the outskirts of Master Data City, and a series of new high-speed roads connecting key towns to the development. It could be a highly lucrative investment for any investor and will enable your government to start making visible progress against this policy. Admittedly, it won't represent quite the scale or pace of change that you'd promised in your manifesto, but it will be a start.

## Is there any money left for innovation?

Your ministers have held some budget back for your final policy area, at your request. You know that, even though the defensive policies are critical to focus on first, if you don't show your voters that you're delivering some things that are really, visibly moving the country forward, they're going to complain.

Whilst some innovation won't possible without the foundations being in place, it's still important to foster a culture of innovation and forward thinking, which is something that can be done even with older data infrastructure. Also, by doing this, it means the country will be more likely to be ready to really take advantage of the new skills and capabilities of its population and improved infrastructure, when they come to fruition.

But you don't have much money to play with, so what will you do?

Once again, it's one of your ministers who comes forward with the ideas. The first idea is to setup a kind of competition, to win grants to deliver new, innovative, value-driving capabilities. This way, the budget can be broken into chunks and can be invested in the best of the business ideas that are put forward. Taking this approach should maximise the chances of a positive return on investment and also generate buzz in the business community, which could lead to other new enterprises as a positive side-effect, without needing to invest in them as well.

The remainder of the funds will then be used for a series of workshops, aimed at data entrepreneurs and businesses, to raise awareness and encourage the business community to drive more innovation.

Once again, this isn't the level of investment that you'd hoped for, but it's a start, and in future years it'll be something that can be built on.

You just hope that what you're doing will be enough…

## Second thoughts

Now you've set things in motion across all aspects of your manifesto, you look back over your decisions. There's no doubt that the ways that you've invested and prioritised changes to laws and enforcement of those laws will drive positive change, but the low levels of investment in transport and infrastructure are bothering you. Have you made the right priority call?

Only time will tell, but at least you know that you made the best decisions you could have made with the information available at the time, so couldn't have done any better than that. No point in worrying about unknown unknowns: it's time to get on with governing your country!

## Actively governing

It's great to finally be in a place where your manifesto has been translated into real, well defined and funded pieces of work, which are now being driven by the various branches of government that have been entrusted with responsibility to deliver the work.

Now it's all running, it's time for you to step away from the detail and into a proper "governing" role.

You've already established clear accountability for each aspect of your manifesto, with a single minister appointed to each policy area. They each report into you, so you establish a series of regular meetings with them to obtain updates and to provide them with leadership and support.

Each minister is responsible for establishing their own local governance arrangements, through whatever structures they deem to be most appropriate, and you do not get involved unless you're asked to. There are a number of sub-committees that you're occasionally invited to attend, but you generally don't need to get too involved.

In order to establish oversight and to coordinate efforts across all policy areas, you establish a new Central Data Government Council, which meets to review progress against all of the new policies, laws and targets. In this council, you summon the ministers responsible for each area and request that they provide updates, then use the council to discuss and agree what needs to be done to provide help where required.

Discussions in your council are often quite high level, but the metrics and regular deep-dives into specific content areas provide you with a level of comfort that the right things are being done, and provides early warning of areas that need more attention and might need interventions to get back on track.

## Only the beginning

You know that this is all only the beginning. Your Data Country has got itself into such a bad state, it's going to take a lot more work than your data population realises to get to a better place, and it'll be a while before you can start to really maximise the value of your data people.

Having said that, you're on the journey and taking those first, important steps. There will no doubt be a range of challenges that you'll face on the way, but your data population are counting on you and the great team that you've assembled. With the strong focus you've placed on the things that matter most to people, you're confident that you're on the path to a totally rejuvenated data economy and data society…

---

**Lesson 2:**
*Data Governance is like running a country. It's crucial to successfully steer a wide range of inter-connected activities that involve a lot of people, and requires experienced leadership, clear communication and coordination, to optimise the value delivered using finite resources.*

---

# 3. THE DATA QUALITY HOSPITAL

**A Data Quality Hospital in crisis…**

The Data Quality Hospital operates within the Data Country, so its patients are all data people.

You've been put in charge of the Data Quality Hospital and it needs your help. There's an overwhelming number of cases flooding in and the numbers seem to be going up. Fears are stirring about a potential data pandemic and something needs to be done to get on top of the ever-increasing volumes of data quality patients.

Data people come to the Data Quality Hospital displaying a variety of different symptoms, so the hospital staff need to act quickly to diagnose the problems and offer appropriate treatments. Some health problems are serious and need urgent treatment to save the data people's lives. When data people die, it's a very upsetting time for their family and friends, which can affect their health too. Also, whilst some health issues don't stop data people from going to work, they can still make them far less effective, and in some cases, they can also put the lives of other data people at risk.

So, it's clearly important to deliver good quality data healthcare, but where do you start…?

**The Triage**

The first thing that data people go through at the Data Quality Hospital is the Triage. It's a rapid assessment that's performed by front-line hospital workers to assess symptoms and make quick decisions about how data patients need to be treated.

If you want to drive improvements to the operation of your hospital, this is a good place to start, because it's the gateway to determining the treatments that will be provided.

There are a few things you're looking out for here: what criteria is being used to prioritise data quality health issues? What's done with patients once they've been prioritised based on their symptoms? Do you have the right people working on the team to deliver the right outcomes and are the processes efficient and effective?

You decide to review the Triage process, starting with the most urgent cases first and have a look at how they're handled.

*Emergency cases*

Data patients with urgent, life-threatening data quality injuries or highly infectious data quality health issues, which could cause problems for other data people, are dealt with as Emergency cases and sent straight to the relevant specialist care unit.

There are also some data patients that attend the hospital who play a particularly important role in society and need to be treated as Emergency patients, receiving an extra level of care to avoid severe or widespread impacts on other data people. These data people are usually identified because they are Critical Data Employees (CDEs). For example, key workers such as data police, data firemen and medical staff are CDEs because if they're not able to do their job, this could have life-threatening consequences for other data people who depend on their services.

At a glance, the criteria for emergency cases all seems sensible; but when you look at the volumes of data people being treated as emergency cases, you see a problem. A backlog of patients is building up because there aren't enough emergency care staff to provide the enhanced care. When you look more closely, you realise that the criteria used to classify someone as a CDE is too long to act as an effective filter: there are so many data people who are being added to the CDE list, it's no wonder the numbers of data people being sent to emergency care is so high.

Also, when you look at the profile of the data quality health conditions being classed as Emergency cases, you realise that the criteria for assessing an injury to be "urgent and life-threatening" is open to interpretation. In particular, a health condition affecting one data person might be life threatening because the data person has an allergy, or because the condition prevents them from fulfilling their role as a CDE; but for another data person, the same condition could be nothing more than an inconvenience.

Your first act to improve the Triage process is to develop more precise guidance about how to classify Emergency cases, which take into account other factors about the data patient, such as underlying health conditions that affect their data patient type and the ways that their condition could affect their ability to fulfil their role as a CDE (if they are one, that is).

However, you are also careful not to artificially skew the emergency assessment, just to reduce demand on emergency staff. You know from experience that an emergency is an emergency, so it would be unethical to de-prioritise some emergency cases by changing the criteria for their assessment, just because you don't have enough people to deal with them. Once the criteria have been appropriately tuned, if your team is still unable to deal with the volumes of cases, then you'll need to look into options for expanding the capacity of the team, including escalating the need for more budget and people, if necessary. The difference is, once you've made the changes, you'll be able to escalate with confidence, because you'll be able to explain the clear rationale for prioritising your emergency cases, plus you'll be able to show what you've done to optimise your team's performance before asking for help.

*Priority cases*

Moving on from the cases that the Triage process have classified as Emergencies, for some data patients, the Triage determines that they're not emergencies, but still need "Priority" treatment, so they are directed to a queue to be dealt with as soon as the relevant data treatment team is available.

Depending on the capacity of the data treatment teams and the number of patients that are being dealt with, the wait can sometimes be a long one. However, sometimes a data person's conditions can deteriorate further when they're waiting, which means they need to be bumped up the queue to be treated more quickly. The staff that look after the queue keep an eye on this and take action when needed. So far, so good.

You take this opportunity to walk around the waiting room and see how Priority cases are being dealt with. There's a small desk, where a busy-looking nurse calls out each data patient's name when it's their turn and tells them which room to go to, in order to receive treatment.

Immediately you can see how things could be improved. Instead of just working through the queue on a totally first-come-first-served basis, the queue could be structured, so that different types of data people, with similar attributes and symptoms, could be grouped into treatment sets, enabling specialists in their conditions to respond to them more quickly and efficiently.

There's also not nearly enough information being tracked about the operation of the priority treatment teams, to provide insight into what's working, what's not working, and trends in health issues. These kinds of insights could inform different approaches to treatments, or more importantly might point to issues outside of the hospital that are causing similar cases occurring, which might be able to be used to develop preventative actions in the community.

You ask for this new information to be gathered and for it to be reported to you weekly. You also arrange regular meetings of priority treatment staff, in order for them to share their experiences amongst each other. You can ask their opinions on how things are running, so that lessons can be learned based on their direct front-line understanding of the realities of the operation of the hospital. You want to start to promote a culture of transparency and collaboration amongst colleagues, to encourage continuous learning and improvement. You know that they will have a better idea of what could be done to practically improve things than you could ever have on your own, so you plan to involve them in the process.

*Non-urgent cases*

Finally, some data patients are assessed as being Non-Urgent. Details about these data patients are logged, but they are then directed to data doctors in their local community to deal with.

Whilst your initial thought is that this group of data patients isn't a major concern, you pause for a moment. What if these people are mis-diagnosed and deteriorate when they return home? What if they come back, with the same symptoms? Would we know?

You've already decided that the Triage prioritisation approach is appropriate, but you also ask for your team to keep an eye on non-urgent cases for follow-up data. For example, from now on, when data people are sent back to their local community data doctors, a message will be sent to their local doctors to inform them that they should expect them to visit, and there is a request to receive an update once they've been seen. This new step is deliberately setup to work with as little effort as possible, for example there isn't a need to actively follow up on every case, but once a month there's a review of the data to see if the hospital has been receiving follow-up messages from local community doctors about non-urgent data people who have been referred with particular symptoms.

The other thing you do, is to add a step to the initial Triage process to check the data person's records to see if they've been in to visit recently, so that repeat visits can be identified, because this could indicate that there's something more serious going on than originally thought and may result in a different Triage decision.

*Organisation*

The Triage process needs to be well structured and coordinated, in order to work properly. The Triage team are experts, with a broad range of experience, who can assess symptoms quickly and make well informed judgements about the best next steps for each patient. You're immediately impressed by the quality of the people and their responsiveness to your questions and suggestions.

The criteria for the team to follow when deciding how patients will be treated, is well documented and is now being improved, so that everyone can be treated fairly and consistently, to increase the likelihood of positive patient outcomes.

Also, the system for record-keeping is being enhanced, to track decisions with audit trails that can be easily accessed and used to manage the process and re-prioritise where necessary.

Once the Triage is completed, there are a range of treatments that can be deployed, depending on the injuries or illnesses that the data patients are suffering with. That's where you turn your focus to next...

**Treating the symptoms**

The first step in many cases is to treat the symptoms. This can be as simple as data cleaning for a wound, applying some cream or giving the data patient some medicine to make them feel better. It's often a fairly superficial first action, but it's often vital to the wellbeing and recovery of the data patient.

Treating the symptoms can make the data patient appear to be much better. In some cases, this is all that's needed. However, in others, although these simple interventions may temporarily alleviate whatever issues the data patient has been experiencing, if they have some other underlying problem that's been causing the symptoms, it's often the case that just cleaning them up only masks the problem and enables them to get back onto their feet for a while, before they're knocked down again.

Treating the symptoms of data quality-related health issues is often a really important task, which has an immediate positive impact. Unfortunately, it's also very rarely enough, and further treatment can be needed to make sure the same patients don't end up back in the near future with the same problems.

Looking at the way this is done, you don't have any immediate concerns, but you know that it's only the start and that on its own, without more effective treatment, it can be a waste of time. If only the symptoms are treated, you're going to be looking at a lot of repeat visits from unhappy data people.

So what next?

## Stopping the bleeding

Sometimes, there can be a problem that's not immediately obviously linked to the data patient's symptoms, which needs to be addressed urgently to stop things becoming worse for them.

For example, a wound could be cleaned up and bandaged, but it may keep on bleeding. Why? Quite often, a closer inspection will uncover the fact that there's a piece of shrapnel in the wound keeping it open, or there's hidden internal bleeding, which isn't visible on the surface. In these cases, the shrapnel need to be removed, the internal bleed needs to be cauterised, and the wounds need stitches to truly stop it from bleeding.

Sometimes, to "stop the bleeding", the data quality medical staff need to look back further into the data patient's life to understand why they keep becoming ill or injuring themselves. Data people are not naturally sickly all on their own: it's their environment and things that happen to them in life or at work that result in injury and illness. As a result, to properly treat an injury, it's important to understand the root cause of it and address that. Otherwise, the data patient may go home and the wound could re-open or the illness could return, and the medical staff will be fighting a never-ending battle of cleaning and bandaging them.

You can sense that you're getting closer to the kinds of actions that will make a real difference in the lives of data patients. Addressing the root cause of a data quality illness clearly needs to be a priority; but what if just stopping the bleeding still hasn't fully resolved the problem? What if there's an infection that is spreading, for which standard treatments aren't working?

## Curing the disease

In some cases, even once the bleeding appears to have been stopped, a data patient may still find themselves with a recurring illness. In these cases, it's likely that the real root cause hadn't been discovered and therefore hadn't been resolved. It's possible that there's something wider or deeper that needs addressing.

To cure a disease means to totally eradicate the disease from the individual. Assuming the data patient doesn't have a chronic, incurable condition that requires ongoing treatment (or a condition that is prohibitively expensive to treat), then it's always preferable to take the time to identify a cure, so that the data patient doesn't ever have to experience the health issues that they have been suffering with again.

Some cures require specialist medicine or surgery, which can be technically challenging and expensive. Depending on the data patient, this might not always be an option, meaning that it's unfortunately more appropriate to continuously treat their symptoms rather than fully curing them. Decisions like this need to be made with the wider prioritisation criteria in mind.

The cases where you can't cure your data patients make you uncomfortable, but you recognise that they're a reality of data healthcare, given the large numbers of different types of data patients, data quality health conditions and treatments that might need to be applied. You keep this in mind when you look towards preventative treatments and what else can be done outside of the hospital. Maybe if more could be done to reduce the likelihood of these incurable diseases from taking hold in the first place, you could improve the chances for large numbers of data patients, resulting in far more data people who are happier and healthier, and leading to far fewer data quality hospital admissions?

## Vaccination and prevention

Once a data patient has been cured, they can go home and won't need to return to hospital. However, if the hospital is encountering a lot of cases of the same illness or injury, the hospital may need to look into what they can do to prevent the illnesses from occurring in the community, because it's far more costly and unpleasant to have to keep dealing with large numbers of ill data people, than if data people can be kept healthy so they can be happy and productive without medical help.

There is a research department in the Data Quality Hospital, which focuses on preventative treatments, such as vaccinations. They study the cases that are coming into the hospital and investigate any that are occurring in large numbers, to see if there's anything that can be done to prevent them from occurring.

There are a range of interventions that they are developing, such as vaccinations and proposed changes to government policy to encourage healthier behaviours or improved safety in the workplace.

Data Vaccinations are one of the most powerful tools in the arsenal of preventative health interventions. Once the root cause of a recurring data health issue has been identified, a data vaccine is developed and rolled out to the population of data people who are most likely to be affected by the disease or other health condition. Very quickly, the Data Quality Hospital sees a significant reduction in the number of those cases, which can be measured through the cases that are coming through the Triage team.

On reviewing the performance of the research team, you identify two things that could be done to help them.

The first is that they only have few people with very specialist knowledge, and a long list of possible projects that they're tackling. In response to this, you decide to recruit two new team members: one with more generalist knowledge, to coordinate the development of experience and expertise across the team; the second with a management background, to help coordinate their efforts so that they can focus on the most important research projects, which deliver the most value.

The second area for improvement is in the relation to the insights the team have on the health of data people. They only receive data from the Triage team, so only get a sense of the known health issues, which data people think are bad enough for them to need to come into hospital. They don't have sight of other health issues that aren't as severe, so they could be missing wider issues or trends, which could be vital in their research.

To help with this, you do two more things. First, you arrange for a regular feed of information from local community doctors on the data health conditions that they are seeing in the community, which can be correlated with your Triage team's view of data quality patients.

Next, you decide to look wider, to see what can be done about monitoring the health of data people in the community...

## Public Data Health Monitoring

When you look into it, it turns out that there's very little public health monitoring being performed. No wonder your research team is struggling to understand what's going on in the community!

Whilst you don't have direct control over public health monitoring, you have some contacts and can pull some strings. You sell the idea that monitoring public health, through both pro-active testing and through monitoring data issues that have been brought to attention, would be an extremely powerful thing to do, in order to help optimise the deployment of medical resources and interventions. You suggest that it will enable the government to make better informed decisions about health policy, spending and interventions.

Of course, for you, it will also help enable the senior leaders in your hospital to better plan and prioritise, both the way in which the hospital operates and also the research and development it performs, based on emerging diseases and health issues.

You manage to obtain some support for some public health monitoring trials, which will test the idea before any decisions about wider or longer-term commitments are made. You're delighted, and keen to show how powerful the insights on the data community will be to enable informed and better decisions.

The trouble is, you know this is only going to bring you insights. It's not going to actually change anything for the better. For this, there's one last thing you want to work on...

## Public Health Advice

If there's one thing you've picked up through your role with this hospital, it's that the general health of the data population is one of the most important factors in reducing the number of health problems and, in particular, the number of admissions to hospital.

As a result, you're delighted to find out that the data government are initiating a new Public Health awareness and advice campaign, aimed at helping people help themselves. You volunteer to help immediately and are optimistic about the results. Helping people help themselves is without a doubt the true path to widespread health improvements (but hard to do!)

## Leading by Example

So what next?

You've reviewed the processes within the hospital and made a number of improvements to drive more effective prioritisation and to start gathering and monitoring data on the effectiveness of the processes, to enable continuous improvements. You've also made some steps to drive better public health, with the hope that this will reduce the number of hospital admissions and generally improve the lives of the data population at large.

This is all great progress, but there's one key thing you still need to do. It's something you've seen the very best health leaders do and now it's your turn: the most important thing you can do now is to role model the behaviours that you're advocating and to "lead by example" – this will be the key that leads to success or failure.

Good luck as you lead the next phase of your hospital's evolution!

---

## Lesson 3:
*Data Quality Management is like running a hospital. Data needs to be healthy (its data quality needs to be maintained), for it to be used for its intended purpose. It's important to implement a dynamic process for diagnosing, prioritising and treating data issues, based on their severity and business value.*

---

# 4. THE DATA ARCHITECTURE CONSTRUCTION PROJECT

## An exciting opportunity... or is it?

You've been waiting for this for a long time. It's the opportunity you've been training for and it's a great honour. After many years of working in various different roles, working your way up the ranks and building experience across numerous positions, you've finally made it. What you don't realise, just yet, is quite what you're getting yourself into.

Three months ago, you successfully completed the build of a new business estate on the outskirts of Master Data City. It used cutting edge new technologies and has become widely recognised as a masterpiece of data engineering. It's become the catalyst for a total transformation of the fortunes of those living and working in the area and prompted a significant increase in investment in similar developments nearby.

Fifty miles North of Master Data City is Data Insight Town, which has been growing rapidly in recent years. There's been a lot of hype in the media about the great opportunities there, and data people from across the Data Country are flocking to make their fortunes amongst the pioneers who have spearheaded the recent new wave of products and services from this emerging powerhouse of value.

The Data Country's government can see the potential of Data Insights Town and have drawn up plans for an infrastructure project that will create a new business hub for innovation and will provide transport links to help data people travel more quickly and comfortably to, from and across the town. It will help people get to work and will also provide them with easier access to data shops and other data amenities, more easily and cheaply than they can get to them today.

You've been appointed as the Chief Architect and Programme Director for the initiative. There are several teams of architects and builders that have been transferred to you to lead and you have a sizeable budget. It's a big responsibility and you can't wait.

Your primary responsibility is to build the new "Data Lakes" development on the far side of Data Insight Town, and to create a high-speed data highway, which will give data people easy access to the new development and its cutting-edge facilities.

There was also a passing mention of the need to tidy up some older parts of the town, where needed, but you've been assured that your focus will be on building the Data Lakes, to spearhead the regeneration of this part of the town and enable the next wave of innovation and business ventures.

## What's going on?!

You're being driven in for your first day by your Head Builder. This is the first time you've been to Data Insight Town, and as you look out at the passing buildings and structures, your jaw drops.

Buildings are crammed together in a total mish-mash of different shapes, sizes and styles. Some look high tech and well maintained and others look half-finished and derelict. At seemingly random intervals, the buildings and roadworks are interspersed with large data garbage heaps, which in some cases are spilling out into the road, slowing data traffic and causing data people to swerve dangerously to avoid them.

One minute you can feel the car gliding along on a nice flat, high quality road, the next you're bumping over makeshift data dirt roads, which act as rough connections from one smooth road surface to another. It's like someone's built a load of separate roads but couldn't join them properly for some reason, so just dug out a path in the dirt as a way to enable data cars to get from one to the next.

You look over at your Head Builder, who looks content and acts as though this is all absolutely fine and normal. You can't believe it. It's the biggest mess you've ever seen. What on earth have you got yourself into?

The other thing that strikes you, looking around, is how much building work seems to be going on. There are cranes, diggers and workmen all over the place. You're pretty sure these aren't members of your team, so you wonder who's commissioned all this work and who's coordinating it.

Then something surprising catches your eye. An imposing structure in the distance, which seems to cut right across the town. It looks like a road on stilts: a huge flyover, carrying data cars from one part of the town to another. You weren't aware of such a flyover and you're sure it wasn't mentioned in any of the briefings.

You ask the Head Builder if you can go and see it. He raises his eyebrows but agrees and takes a slip road in its direction.

What you're about to find is more bizarre than you could possibly have imagined...


## The sticky-plaster data bridge

As you draw closer to the structure, you can see that it's covered in what appears to be large plasters and bandages. You rub your eyes in disbelief. They literally look like the kinds of plasters you'd use if you grazed your knee, but blown up to a much bigger size and plastered all over it.

You want to get a closer look, so ask: "Can you take me to the base of the structure, please?"

The Head Builder nods in response to your request. "Boss, if you don't mind me asking, why are you interested in coming down here? Don't you just want to get to your office? That's what all the other architects normally do."

You smile at the suggestion that you'd allow yourself to fall into that stereotype. "I need to see what's actually going on, because otherwise I'm not going to know if our plans are practical or not."

"Oh, OK. I just thought you were an architect, that's all."

You hold back a laugh. "I am an architect!"

"But don't architects just stay in their office drawing pictures?" You can't tell whether your new colleague is joking or not, but if he's not, you can see why your predecessors may have failed to deliver very much.

At this point, you've arrived at the base of the flyover and you decide to continue your conversation later. It's going to be important for people to understand the role you're going to be playing and how everyone's going to have to work together, but if your Head Builder's thinking this way, it's going to take more than a five-minute chat.

You both get out of the car and look up at the patchwork structure. "Do you know what's underneath the plasters?"

The Head Builder shakes his head. "I couldn't be absolutely sure. We think it's old data pipework, but the people that built it retired a few years ago and we only have people who know how to tend to the plasters. Trouble is, the plasters themselves are now so inter-twined, there's only a handful of people who know how to maintain them now, too."

"Wow." What you're looking at is both a crazy marvel of engineering and a maintenance nightmare.


## Don't worry about the data losses

What happens next is the most shocking and scary thing you've ever seen.

There is a sudden, loud crashing noise above you. When you look up, you find yourself frozen to the spot, as a data car tumbles from the highway and plummets down a hole only three feet from where you're standing. You feel the rush of air caused by the data car plunging past you, and watch in horror as the data person inside screams in terror before disappearing into oblivion.

You're gasping for breath as you look at the Head Builder and are stunned to see him gazing at you quizzically. He looks totally nonplussed by what he's just seen.

"What," you wheeze, "just happened?!"

"Oh that? That's nothing. I mean, it's normal. I mean, it's pretty rare, in the grander scheme of things. Considering how many data cars use the flyover, it's pretty amazing that so few are lost."

Before you have a chance to reply, there's another crashing sound, and you jump backwards as another car plummets past you and down the hole.

"Where do they go?"

"Oh, we don't exactly know, but there's no getting them back, that's for sure. Once they're lost down that hole, they're gone for good."

You can't believe how relaxed he's being about this. It's like it's a totally normal occurrence. But that was a data person in there, you could see the fear in their eyes, and now they're gone! That can't be right!

"Hasn't anything been done to stop that from happening?"

"Oh yes, yes. We've got a team of people up there, watching out for data cars that might go missing. When one of them looks like it's going to go off track, the team jumps to action and uses a belt of sticky plasters to nudge them in the right direction. Nine times out of ten, it works, too."

"You have a team of people looking out for data car crashes and then manually redirecting data cars when they go off track?"

"Yep."

"But wouldn't it make more sense just to fix the data highway, so that none go missing?"

The Head Builder snorts. "Well, yeah, but that'd cost a lot and no one wants to spend that kind of money, given that our team catches most of the cars that go over there."

As if on cue, another car rushes past. There's a whole family of data people in this one and their cries for help ring in your ears.

"Surely employing a full-time team and having to keep buying plasters is expensive?"

"Oh yeah, I mean, it's not cheap, but it's cheaper than actually fixing the flyover properly, and it's not like many data people go missing, so it's alright."

"Not many...?" You stop as you realise, looking at your Head Builder's face, he is totally convinced that there's nothing to worry about. Now you're worried. What else has been built like this? What other dodgy manual fixes are you going to find?

You've seen enough here, so ask to be taken to your office. As you're driven there, you think through what you're going to say to your new team and wonder how they're going to react. You decide to start by asking questions and listening…

## "What a team!" Or should that be… "What team?"

A meeting's been organised with the leaders of each of your teams. Helpfully, representatives from some of the other architecture firms and building companies have also agreed to join.

As you walk into the meeting room, you can feel the tension amongst the people gathered there. You smile broadly and say hello, walking in with as much confidence as you can muster to take a seat at the top of the long table that fills most of the room. The windows are open, but there's no breeze and the room's hot and stuffy. All of the seats are occupied, people crammed into the narrow gaps between the table and the walls, and there are a few people stood up at the back of the room. You can see one person leaning on the limp remains of a broken fan, wafting himself with a notebook in a vain attempt to cool down.

You introduce yourself and offer your vision of positive collaboration and collective success. Rather than spending lots of time talking about yourself, you make it clear that you want to hear from people in the room and invite them to speak in turn. You say that you're keen to encourage open discussion and want to hear about people's concerns and challenges, so you can do something about them.

*Abstraction Utopia*

The team to go first is sat closest to you and is clearly keen to impress. It's the Strategic Architecture team. The team's leader eagerly introduces himself and his three team members, who are surrounded by stacks of printouts and as they start talking, are pointing at some very pretty-looking presentation slides displayed on their sleek tablet computers.

This is the kind of Architecture team that your Head Builder had been talking about. Lots of great ideas and pretty pictures, but the diagrams and strategies that they describe to you have very little connection to reality.

The vision that they paint envisages the use of the most advanced technologies to deliver transformational value to all who use them. Everything will fit into the neat concepts that the boxes on their slides represent, and data will flow seamlessly and without error from one end of the page to the other. It's inspiring and expansive. It's compelling thought leadership and you can see the excitement and hope in their eyes.

It's also totally unrealistic.

They clearly understand technology and have definitely done their research into the newest and best tools available. You can also tell that this is a team of technology experts who really know the state of the art and could have some great, out-of-the-box ideas to solve problems, if they were directed at the right problems to solve and with the right constraints. Unfortunately, they've spent too long gazing at the stars and thinking into the future, without being grounded in the current challenges so that they could develop solutions to immediate problems and work out what needs to happen in the "here and now", to be able to get to the "there and then".

To be fair to them, they do finish off their presentation by skimming through fifty pages of "transition state" plans, with beautiful illustrations, showing how their vision could be realised by building the new structures on top of the remnants of the legacy architectures across Data Insights Town. The trouble is, although you can appreciate the theory, you also know from what you saw on your drive to the office, that the theory isn't based on a real understanding of the existing architectures or what it's going to take to evolve the town in a realistic and cost-effective way.

You thank the team encouragingly and give the nod for the next team to talk.

*Technology Snobs*

The next representative to speak clears his throat before he starts. He's not joined by anyone else from his team and commences by announcing with a distinct air of pride that he leads the Infrastructure Maintenance team. His team is responsible for the upkeep of critical infrastructure and they directly protect the safety of everyone travelling and using the facilities across Data Insight Town.

It turns out that the Infrastructure Maintenance team employs over two thousand infrastructure engineers, including a few of the only people that still understand some of the old materials and technologies that have been used to build the town.

Initially you're impressed. This team seems to be everything the Strategic Architecture team isn't: it's practical, delivery-focused and has a very strong sense of how it delivers value.

However, alarm bells begin ringing in your head at some of the things the Head of Infrastructure Maintenance is saying. The team is highly reactive. They jump into action when they hear something's going wrong, rushing to prop up old data structures and plug gaps in data roads. They are the sticky plaster experts and don't seem to have any idea about the condition of the structures across the town and how fast they're deteriorating, so aren't able to plan or do anything pro-active or preventative.

Also, you sense a real sense of nostalgic attachment to some of the old technologies. The Head of Infrastructure Maintenance's monologue is peppered with comments that are dismissive of the Strategic Architecture team's previous presentation and their lack of connection to the "real world". There's clearly no love lost between these two teams.

You ask about what alternative approaches and tools they've considered to improve the sustainability of their fixes, and the defensive reaction tells it all. They love the technologies they use and other technologies couldn't possibly be any better. They're also world experts in them. The only experts left, because some of the technologies are on their way to extinction!

As with the previous team, you make it clear that you're happy that they've been so candid and forthright with their views, before moving to the next team.

*The Executors*

The next person to step forward is sharply dressed, and as she starts to talk, her calm, commanding tone is precise and crisp. Her eyes are intense and focused. The description of her team's purpose, its achievements and plans are structured, logical and well-rehearsed.

This is the Programme Delivery team. Their job is to "get stuff done". They don't have any preference of technologies or tools, they just need to know what needs to be done, by when, and with what resources, and they'll make sure it happens.

Their team is very new and consists of expert delivery managers, brought in from other towns and cities. It was set up following the various overdue and unsuccessful projects that the incumbent teams had failed to get over the line. The team leader is almost jarringly direct and doesn't hesitate to explain the issues with cross-team working, lack of budgetary control, absence of leadership and unwillingness to collaborate. You can see people from other teams wincing and crossing their arms as she talks. Whilst you're really glad to hear such honest feedback, it's not delivered in the most diplomatic way, and the team's going to need to work well with the other people in the room, so you can see there's going to need to be a bit of work put into relationship building here.

Having said that, it's a relief to know that you have people with delivery skills, even if the team is small, new and currently a little disconnected. It's increasingly evident that you're going to have your work cut out encouraging these various groups of people to work together productively, but you know it's better to have that problem, than to have lots of people who all get on well but don't have the skills you need to get the work done.

One thing that does concern you slightly, as you listen to the concluding remarks, is some of the comments you've heard about delivery being "the only thing that matters". Whilst delivery is crucial, it's also important to care about the way in which things get done, the outcomes and the people affected. Then again, if this team really is as good as their leader is saying they are, then they should know that.

You thank your Head of Programme Delivery and move onto the next team.

*Concerned Contractors*

The next set of people to speak turn out to be a group of external contractors, who are there to represent a number of other external architecture and building companies. They work for private investors but are keen to ensure they have good working relationships with your government-backed team. It turns out that they have some concerns of their own too, which they're all too happy to share with you.

The contractors aren't shy about their motives. They make it very clear that in most cases, they'll do whatever they're told, as long as they're paid enough. However, they struggle when they're asked to do something they don't agree with, because they're all experienced professionals and have standards of their own. They don't want to put their name to something that's sub-par and they make every effort to steer their clients in the right direction. In some cases, they tell you, they have refused to do certain things, because they're downright unsafe. The trouble is, there's always another company that's happy to pick up your contract if you walk out on it.

You're told stories of projects where the private investors have spent so much money on them, they don't want to admit failure so keep on going, even when their contractors have told them that it would be more sensible and cost effective to cut their losses and try a different approach.

You also hear about several projects that were abandoned half-way through because funds dried up or investors lost their nerve, but where there was no interest in wrapping up the build properly, resulting in partially-built safety hazards left in the middle of the town.

The other thing you learn is that the only contractors in the room are the ones who actually want to be there. There are some "cowboy" contractors, who are just out to make some quick money, without caring about the consequences of their shoddy work. These cowboys couldn't be bothered to turn up today and the contractors who are presenting to you now share their worries that these other rogue builders are giving them a bad name and making everyone's lives harder by making the town's architecture more complex and more fragile than it needs to be.

You're surprised to hear that some of this is even possible. Back when you were working in Master Data City, there were strict data building regulations that needed to be adhered to and were policed by the local Data City Architecture Councils. You make a note that you'll need to talk to Data Insight Town's governor, to see if something similar would be possible to arrange here. Without properly enforced building regulations, you could end up fighting a losing battle against dodgy buildings and hard-to-maintain infrastructure, even if you are successful in getting your own teams to work in better ways.

By the time the contractors have finished, they look exhausted. You can tell how much stress they're under and it was clearly a cathartic experience for them to share their worries.

*Your Build Team*

Now that you've heard from everyone else, you return your attention to your Head Builder, who's sat calmly in his chair next to you. As he starts to talk, you're surprised to notice an immediate shift in the atmosphere of the room. Arms are uncrossed, frowns are relaxed, attentions are re-focused and the previously stifling temperature seems to tangibly drop and feel more bearable. He starts by thanking his peers and some of the other people who've spoken, who turn out to be former colleagues of his, for their introductions. Then he offers a bit of background before he goes into his team's current role and what they're doing at the moment.

Your Head Builder first came to Data Insights Town as a teenager and joined one of the earliest building teams as an apprentice. He talks fondly of the high standards, pride and work ethic of the pioneers that built the town. As the town grew and the local council took a more active role in overseeing its development, he moved to join the new organisation that would eventually become the team that you see before you.

Back then, the senior Architecture and Delivery leaders were experts in their field, who had been appointed into their positions due to the central roles they had played in leading many of the ground-breaking developments that established Data Insight Town. They understood how to design and build structures that were cost-effective and fit for purpose. They pushed the boundaries through the sensible use of new technologies, whilst being careful to only do so when it made sense and delivered value.

The success of the team led to its rapid expansion. Your Head Builder rose through the ranks and was fortunate enough to work with a range of great people. As he speaks, he indicates to some of the people sat around the table, who smile and nod in positive acknowledgement of their shared past.

The changes in the fortunes of the team started when some of the senior leaders were headhunted to join large firms in other cities away from Data Insights Town. New executives were brought in, who didn't have the same level of experience or standards as their predecessors. Their focus was on saving money on "non-essential" activities such as quality control, in favour of "value-driving" developments, such as new Data Storage Warehouses and Data Insight Marts. They were frustrated by the speed of delivery and removed some of the minimum requirements that had been in place for all buildings in the past, in an attempt to speed things up.

Your Head Builder shakes his head, as he recounts a time when he escalated his concerns because a data office building was being built on a swamp with no foundations. His escalation was ignored. He was called a "purist" and "impractical".

"… But anyone who knows anything about good data architecture, knows that you need good foundations if you want to do anything!" There are lots of nods from people around the room, as your Head Builder says this. You can sense the respect they all have for him and wonder if you were a bit too quick to judge him, based on what you saw on your drive into the office.

Needless to say, he tells you, the results of this change of approach were disastrous. Then the blame game started. First, the project management teams were all fired, because there was a perception that they weren't working, due to the issues with delivery. The Building team was expected to absorb this capability as well as doing the all of the building work they had been doing before.

Next, the Architecture team was fired. The executives felt that the architects were too expensive and didn't have anything to add that their experienced builders couldn't do. The Architects had previously maintained all of the schematics and plans for the whole town, but once they were gone, the plans fell quickly out of date and projects were initiated based on the whim of business executives without any real idea of how they would fit into the wider landscape.

As things continued to worsen, the next idea executives came up with, was to get help from more private companies, rather than depend on the government-backed teams. The Head Builder's boss was poached by one of the big contracting firms that was brought in and that was how he ended up being promoted into his current position.

It was around this time that the accidents started occurring. Data cars started disappearing down holes, the first set of data structures fell over and data warehouses fell into disrepair, overflowing with garbage and leaking corrupt data mess into the adjoining streets.

Many data people's lives were lost. Before this time, there hadn't been a need for a sizeable maintenance team, but now it was clear that it was essential. In order to rapidly mobilise this new capability, some of the best people from the Data Build team were transferred into a newly expanded Infrastructure Maintenance team.

Since this all happened, over the past few years, your Head Builder has done his best to keep things going as best he could. He's lost good people to other teams and to contracting companies that pay more, but those who are still working for him are experienced and very loyal. The way things have been organised has made it difficult for him to be as effective as he could have been, but with his colleagues he's still managed to deliver some successful builds.

The Build team is much smaller than it used to be, but your Head Builder is proud to be in charge of a set of master builders, who work on the most important building projects and provide support to other teams whenever needed. They operate a bit like an internal consultancy service and have a mix of architecture, project management and practical building skills. They also know a fair amount about the history of the town and have relationships with most of the other organisations working there.

As the Head Builder finishes his speech, he waits for a moment and allows the silence to linger. Then he smiles broadly and his next set of words are gentle and reassuring. "So, as you may have noticed, there are a number of us here, who care quite a lot about this town. We've all been through some pretty frustrating times in recent years, but I'd like to hope that I can speak for everyone in this room when I say that we all want to do the best work we can and to turn Data Insight Town into the kind of place all data people want to come to visit and work and live."

Now that you've heard from everyone, you have a pretty good idea of the strengths and weaknesses of your teams and how they'll need to work together to be effective. It's obvious that you'll need more time than just this afternoon to work out all of the details, but you want to lay the groundwork immediately.

You thank everyone again and ask them to come back in a couple of hours to have a forward-looking discussion.

As the room clears, you reflect on what you've just heard and how you're going to run the follow-up meeting in the afternoon. There's a range of challenges that you're going to need to overcome, but you're feeling far better than you had been earlier. If anything, you can feel a cautious excitement rising within you. Although there's a lot that needs to be done to foster trust and communication amongst these teams, there is an unquestionably diverse set of skills and experience across these groups of people, which could prove to be very powerful. Now you just need to work out how to harness all of that potential, in a practical and useful way.

**A new regime**

When everyone returns, you start by playing back some of the points that you've heard. You acknowledge frustrations and concerns, before drilling down into some of the changes that you'll be making to the way everyone works, which you'd like to implement as soon as possible.

The structure of the teams and their leaders will stay as they are for now, to minimise disruption, but there will be a weekly meeting scheduled, where all of those present in the room today, including the contractors, will gather and collaborate, from this point forwards. This group will start to act as a joined-up leadership team, and that means that everyone will support each other and prioritise shared objectives over any goals that teams have individually. This may take some time to get right, and that's OK: the main thing will be to start thinking of each other as being part of a bigger whole. You invite people to be open and free to speak their mind, so that issues can be identified and dealt with quickly.

**Pragmatic Data Architecture**

Turning to the Data Architects, you praise their vision and enthusiasm. Your plan for them is to involve them more directly with the work that all of the other teams are delivering, so their role can become more pragmatic. This should dramatically increase the chances of delivering the more advanced tools and technologies that they have been researching.

In order to facilitate this change, the Architects' time will need to be divided between four activities.

- The first, most important activity, will be to use their design expertise to review the current plans that Build and Infrastructure Maintenance teams are delivering, to either help them improve by suggesting alternative ways of designing things, or to endorse them so that everyone can have more confidence that the projects that are being delivered are making the town's architecture better. You look around the room and ask that the other teams are open to the Architects' help. This is all about starting to work better together and benefitting from each other's different skillsets. This first task will mean that the Architects will be involved in the design phase of all new projects, so their expertise will be used practically. It will mean that project teams can learn from them, and they can learn more about the practical realities of how the town is currently setup.

- The second task that you want the Architects to take on will be even more dependent on support from the other teams. You want them to start developing a set of schematics that reflect the known current state of the town's infrastructure and buildings. Every time a project delivers something new, it will be up to them to submit their architectural drawings and plans to the Architecture team, for them to add it to their knowledgebase, which will then help better inform designs and plans for future developments. Involving the Architects in the design phase of projects will also help with this, but they may not have capacity to work on every project so the responsibility will be with delivery teams to submit the content to the Architects, and

49

the Architects will then maintain them.

- The third responsibility that you give the team is to start drafting and formalising a set of building regulations. You offer to provide them with contacts in Architecture teams in other cities to help fast-track this exercise with some tried-and-tested requirements and design patterns. Many building regulations are based on the same core principles around data structure design and upholding the safety of data people when they're using the structures, but you're keen for the Architects to utilise their expertise to develop standards and rules that help everyone working in the town to deliver better and safer buildings.

- Finally, you still want the team to continue to invest some of their time in researching and experimenting with new technologies. The passion for innovation and the art of the possible is really important for the future of the town. It's exciting and could open up opportunities that currently seem beyond reach, so it's something you're keen to maintain. However, the other tasks must take priority, so you suggest that they forward-book time to spend on this, to make sure other priorities don't get in the way.

You can tell from the reactions around the room that not everyone is convinced by your proposals, so you re-iterate the point you've already made about how important it will be for everyone to be open and share their concerns, and that it will be through collaborating as a team and learning that everyone will succeed. If something isn't working, that's fine, we'll work out why it isn't and adjust.

*Pro-active Maintenance*

Turning your attention to the Head of Infrastructure Maintenance, you confirm to him that you know that there is still a need to react to urgent maintenance needs, especially where the safety of data people is at risk.

However, building on what you've just said about the Strategic Architecture team, you would like the Architects to be involved in any significant maintenance works, because there may be opportunities to use new technologies and techniques, to improve the longevity of repairs and also make them easier to maintain and build on in the future.

Before there's a chance for a disagreement to be raised about this, you hold up your hand and continue assertively. You respect and appreciate the expertise of the people who have been using tried-and-tested technologies for a long time. You are not dismissing their value and you just want the right solutions to be implemented for the right jobs. If old technologies are the right things to use, then they should be used. However, if they're not, then it's important to be honest with ourselves about this and to consider better alternatives. By involving the Architects, the Infrastructure team can teach them about the old technologies, so they can learn the best ways to use them, and at the same time, the Architects can teach the Infrastructure team about new tools and techniques, so they can be upskilled and be even more useful and effective in the future. If both teams enter into this with open minds, it will be a win-win scenario for everyone involved.

Next, you address the reactive nature of the team and how important it is to be more proactive. Whilst responding to emergencies is undoubtedly critical for the health and wellbeing of data people using the town, doing everything this way is inefficient and unsustainable. The team will be under far more stress working in this way and they could also end up missing important opportunities because they're so busy just dealing with the tasks immediately in front of them. In order to help with this, you'll be asking the Programme Delivery team to provide support and would like to encourage the Infrastructure team be open to their advice and guidance.

Finally, in order to support the more pro-active management of the data infrastructure across the town, you would like the team to start reporting on the condition of the data structures that they're fixing, and also to start monitoring the data people and data cars that are using the infrastructure. Without knowing the condition of the data structures and how they are being used, it will be impossible to know which ones need the most attention and why.

There's a bit of a pause, as you observe the reactions around the room again. You can still see some concern on some people's faces, but there's been a lot less resistance than there could have been, and no-one's actually complained yet. You take a breath and continue.

*Transparent, Integrated Delivery Support*

Speaking to the entire room, you take a moment to share how impressed you are with the expertise that you can tell exists within and across teams. You acknowledge that there have been challenges with delivery in the past, but this has been in part due to a range of factors that were not entirely within the control of the people assembled here today.

Now there's an opportunity for everyone to take back control and to deliver more successfully together. This is where you see the Programme Delivery team playing a pivotal role.

Effective delivery is important for all teams. As such, members of the Programme Delivery office will need to embed themselves within each team, to act as trusted partners in establishing good practice project management and cross-team collaboration. They will not be there to lead the delivery themselves, because that's still the accountability of the leaders of each team, but they will be there to support and help steer.

Also, crucially, they will establish transparent reporting on status and progress, which will be reported back to this leadership team every week, so that everyone understands what's going on, across all areas. You want to hear about risks and issues early, so that action can be taken, and will be far more forgiving of people who admit that they're struggling, than people who try sort out all of their problems by themselves, without sharing them with this group. "We're all in this together. We're one team, here to support each other to succeed collectively."

At this point, you can see your Head of Programme Delivery is sat forward in her chair. You maintain your composure and nod positively in her direction. Despite the fervour, you know this is going to be a more challenging culture shift than your words make it sound, but success will be achieved through the practical application of this new way of working, day by day, and through consistent "leadership by example". Enthusiasm is a very good starting point for this.

*External Partners*

Turning now to the group of Contractors, you thank them again for being so open with their observations, and state your intention to engage them pro-actively by making them part of the extended leadership team. You acknowledge the fact that they are independent and their loyalty will rightly be with their private investors. You also point out that there will be some activities and discussions that they will not be able to be part of, due to their external role, but at a minimum, they'll have a seat at the weekly leadership team meetings.

By involving them directly, you're keen to hear their candid views on what's happening across the rest of the town, what's working and not working, as early as possible. Doing this will also mean that they will get to hear about, and in some cases influence, initiatives that are being managed by this team.

Referring back to the concerns that they raised earlier about unsafe data practices, you inform them of your intention to talk to the Data Insight Town's governor, to take steps to address this formally.

*Build Team*

Getting back to your Head Builder, you're pleased to announce that you've spoken to him this afternoon and he will be formally taking on the role of your deputy. He smiles and nods, and you can see the look of approval from people around the room.

As such, people should feel free to come to either you or him if they have any questions or concerns. You'll be working together to make sure that everyone in this new leadership team is connected and supported. The Build Team will continue to be engaged across teams, as it has been previously, prioritising their effort based on the areas of greatest need.

## The challenges ahead

Now that you've laid out your plans for the way you'd like the team to work, you give people a few minutes to allow what you'd said to sink in, before you wrap up the meeting with a summary of next steps.

This is just the beginning and through active collaboration and regular reflection on the operational performance of the team, the operating model is something that can be evolved over time, based on the lessons that are learned along the way.

Whilst you do believe that the changes you've outlined will help everyone work better together and will by implication drive greater productivity and success, it's also important that everyone is clear on the challenges ahead and the part that each individual plays in addressing them.

Data Insights Town is very busy, with many data people travelling across it and using its facilities every day. Any building work will cause disruption and will put some data people at risk. There will be times when parts of the transport network needs to be temporarily shut to enable maintenance work, or where data people will need to be re-directed, especially when new roads are opened up.

Data people will always need to travel and they will find a way to get across town to work, even if they have to work around the infrastructure that's in place in circuitous, costly and unsafe ways. This is a reality that needs to be accepted and considered when delivering data building projects.

Everyone has become very used to ways of working that are going to need to change, and that's going to be challenging at first. It's going to take conscious effort and the support of each other to make those changes stick.

To name a few simple examples: the constant use of sticky-plasters is no longer acceptable. Although it will be tolerated where absolutely necessary, it's important to start designing for the future, using the right materials for the right job.

It will no longer be acceptable to build without establishing the right foundations first. This will add time and cost up-front, but will speed things up in the long run. There'll also be a shift to more modular, re-usable structures. This will make them faster to build, easier to extend and connect together.

Whilst all of this sounds very straightforward, you know it's going to mean change for people, which will require support and follow-through.

The final point you want to make is about keeping the end user in mind. Everything is being built for data people, and the way that they will derive value from the roads and buildings that are being built and maintained, will be through using them. This needs to be front and centre during every build: why do data people need these new structures and how will they be designed and built to deliver the most value for them and to encourage them to use them?

In terms of next steps, you've now laid out your initial thoughts on how you'd like the teams to work differently. You'll be arranging for the weekly meetings to be established from next week, along with regular one-to-one catch-ups with each member of the leadership team. You ask that each team lead considers what they've heard and pulls together a plan for how they intend to implement the new ways of working.

On this note, you're finished for today. You thank everyone for joining and express your sincere excitement for this opportunity and the privilege to lead such a great team. You're looking forward to working with such a talented group of people and are confident that by working as a well-coordinated group, you will all be very successful.

**Hope for the future**

After the meeting has finished, your Head Builder finds you back in the meeting room, leaning back in your chair and gazing out of one of the windows at the Data Insights Town skyline. The sun is setting behind one of the tall buildings in the distance and the sky is awash with hues of red, yellow and orange.

His presence stirs you from your reverie and you look at him with a smile. "How do you think my first day went?"

"Could've been worse," comes the response, with a chuckle.

You laugh in return. "That sounded enthusiastic!"

Your new deputy comes and sits next to you. He speaks slowly and with meaning. "I'll be honest, Boss. Things haven't been great around here for a long time. I think you can see that from what you've heard today. But you can also see how much everyone here cares about this town. We're all here to make things better. That's why we came here in the first place. We've had lots of people come here with their big ideas and mess things up, but today you showed that you could listen and you want the best for us. That means a lot, and if you really do mean what you say, and really do follow through on it, then all I can say is that I'll do everything I can to help."

What a long way you've come, in just one day. You look at your new companion seriously when you reply. "I meant every word of it. I can see we've got some great people here and I'm looking forward to working with you to deliver some great things."

Nothing more needs to be said. The journey has begun. Together, you're going to transform Data Insights Town for the better.

---

**Lesson 4:**
*Data Architecture is like delivering a large infrastructure building project. Connecting good design theory to practical delivery, and coordinating the efforts of multiple delivery and maintenance teams, can make the difference between a costly mess and amazing success.*

---

# 5. THE METADATA MESS

**A new job**

You've been called in to help. You've not taken on a job quite this big before, but it's your area of specialism: retail troubleshooting. In other words, you're a consultant who helps improve the performance of data shops and retail outlets.

The retail chain that's contacted you is the biggest in the country: the "Multi-Data Mart". They have shops on every data high street and they sell a wide range of data products. They've been big for decades, but over recent years, customer satisfaction levels have been dropping and now they're in trouble. It'll be your job to work out what's been going wrong and to help with their turnaround, if you can.

As always, the best place to start is on the frontline: in the shops themselves. One of the smaller shops in their chain is just ten minutes away from where you live, so you arrange to meet the store manager in the morning.

**Checking out at the checkout**

When you first walk in, everything looks pretty normal. Like many other shops, you can see a series of aisles, stretching back in rows towards the rear of the building, with products stacked on shelves up to your eye level.

Then you notice something that does seem a bit different. There are only a handful of customers in the shop, but despite this, there is a scene of panic and chaos at the checkout. There's an assistant who is visibly flustered, making frantic, apologetic gestures in the face of a clearly agitated customer. Behind the customer, a queue is forming.

You walk over to find out what's going on.

"I'm sorry, sir, if you look on the side of the box, you can see that I've got you the data product that you asked for."

The customer isn't having any of it. "Who cares what it says on the box, if the contents are something completely different? This is totally useless to me. I'm glad I didn't try to use it, it could have caused me an injury!"

The customers in the queue are shaking their heads. It looks like they're all there to return data products, too. When you look back at the checkout, the assistant has gone into a back room to see if they can find the data product that the customer had actually asked for.

Then you notice someone sheepishly waving at you from the back of the store. It's the store manager, who clearly doesn't want to be seen by any of the customers. Discretely wandering away from the scene at the checkout, you make your way over and introduce yourself.

"Thank goodness you're here," the store manager exclaims, as she guides you towards the stockroom, "I can't put up with much more of this. It's an embarrassment and it's not our fault!"


## Metadata mix-up

When you get to the stockroom, the store manager turns to you abruptly. "What you saw just there is happening all the time. No matter what we do, we keep getting it wrong. It's embarrassing. We know it's because the metadata labels are wrong, but they're wrong when they come into the store so we don't stand a chance!"

You ask her to show you some examples. "Just take your pick. It's a mess." Going over to the first box you see, you open it up and are immediately confused. You look up at the description on the rack, then down at the products in the box.

"This product's in the wrong place," you say.

The store manager shakes her head. "Open up one of the products and have a look what's inside."

You do just that, and discover that the data product within is totally different to the label on the outside. You look up at the sign on the shelf and it matches the actual data product, within its mis-labelled packaging.

"We've been trying to organise things onto shelves based on what's actually in the boxes, not based on what's on their packaging. When we first realised that the metadata labels were all wrong, we started doing that so we could still find them, but then we started receiving stock that was even more mixed up and it's been getting worse ever since."

The store manager slumps onto a hard, plastic chair that's next to one of the stacks of shelves and sighs. "I've been working here for over ten years and used to know where everything was and how to give the customer exactly what they wanted. Now, when a customer asks us to get something from the stockroom, it takes us ages to find it, we have to double-check the contents to make sure they match the packaging, and even then, things still go wrong. It takes us twice as long to unload new stock from the lorries into the warehouse because we can't trust the labels so we have to check everything manually. I've always taken pride in the customer service this store provides and now I'm ashamed to work here. It's just terrible."

You nod and express your understanding. You can tell the store manager is a committed, diligent worker. She's been trying her best to get things right, going above and beyond, and has been struggling against the rubbish she's been receiving.

You're going to need to go further up the supply chain to find out the cause of these problems. You thank the store manager and obtain the details of the main distribution centre. It's called the Central Data Warehouse and you head straight there.


**The shiny façade of the Central Data Warehouse**

As you drive up to the Data Warehouse, you can't help but marvel at its scale. The imposing structure looms above you as you navigate your way towards the vast parking area that's been cordoned off for visitors. The other thing that strikes you is how high-tech it looks. This isn't just a rusty old building filled with data products; or at least, from the outside it doesn't look like it is. If anything, the architecture of the building is surprisingly sleek, with a tasteful mix of glass and metal that radiates a proud sense of thoughtful, cutting-edge design. No expense was spared in creating this structure, that's for sure.

As you enter the spacious lobby, you see a sharp-looking figure striding towards you. The man before you is wearing a pristine, fitted suit and has slick black hair. As he approaches, he flashes a gleaming bleach-white smile and confidently holds out his perfectly manicured hand. "Welcome," he purrs, "to the Central Data Warehouse."

His handshake is as firm and well-practiced as his intro. "I'm the Head of Warehousing Solutions and I've been asked to give you the tour. It'll be my pleasure to show you around. I'm sure you'll be impressed with our world-leading facility."

*Head of Solutions*, you think, smiling inside, *more like Head of Sales*. You're used to meeting people like this. They're all about the image of the place and are great for positive PR, but often don't have much depth of understanding about day-to-day operations, beyond the buzzwords and straplines that they spout. You'll give him the benefit of the doubt though, as it's always best to enter into conversations with an open mind.

"Right this way," indicates your guide warmly, and you follow him through the expensive-looking automatic turnstiles towards a large set of glass sliding doors, which sweep open when the Head of Solutions advances towards them. "The doors know it's me because they automatically detect my biometric signature," he boasts.

You smile encouragingly, also noticing the various CCTV cameras and other fancy security gizmos that are installed throughout the building. *Interesting that he hasn't asked my name yet though*, you think. You were able to freely walk through those turnstiles without signing in or anything. All these technical security features look great, but if you don't do the basics, they're nothing but window dressing.

At the end of the corridor, you are presented with rows of what look like high-tech golf buggies, with various sizes of trailers attached to them. The warehouse is far too big to get around on foot, so these transport vehicles must be how people travel to the places they need to get to. As you climb into the passenger side of one of the data transports, which has "SQL01" printed across its door, the Head of Solutions turns to you and asks you where you want to go first.

"I'd like to see how data products are shipped from here to shops."

"Great place to start," comes the reply, as a series of commands are typed into a touchscreen in the transport buggy's cockpit. "Every part of this warehouse is indexed," he explains, "so I'm typing a command for this transport to select the right location to take us to. I'll be taking you to the distribution port."

As he presses 'enter', you are surprised by a strange feeling that comes over you, almost like you're being stretched. You instinctively squeeze your eyes shut as the transport makes a gentle "shhh" sound, and when you open them, you're stunned to see that you're in a totally different room.

Disoriented and blinking like you've just had a bright light shone in your face, you turn to see the Head of Data Solutions grinning at you. "It's awesome, isn't it?" he enthuses. "We've developed this technology specifically for our warehouses, so we can rapidly access the data products we need and get them to where we need them. What you've just experienced is nothing: we can select groups of products from multiple parts of the warehouse and join them together into a single package, almost instantaneously, which we can then ship to various destinations from the distribution port here. We can automate whatever we need to as well, of course. This facility has some of the most advanced data product management logistics and orchestration technologies in the world."

Like everything else in this warehouse, the distribution port is massive. You're parked on a viewing platform, overlooking rows and rows of lorry bays, which go out as far as the eye can see. Down below is a hive of activity. Data products are being beamed in using transport buggies like the one you've just travelled in and robotic forklift trucks are loading them onto lorries. The lorries are driving in, being loaded up and setting off. There are so many of them, moving in rapid, fractal-like patterns, that it looks like some kind of complicated mechanical dance. The system is clearly highly sophisticated and processing large volumes of data products, at pace.

"Once you've shipped a set of data products, how do you find out if there are any issues with them?" you ask.

"Oh, there won't be any issues with our data products," the Head of Data Solutions says dismissively. You can see that he immediately regrets the slip: "What I mean to say is, we have such strong automated quality control, we've totally removed the chance of any errors."

"Are you saying there's no way for stores that receive your deliveries to feedback, if they have any issues?"

The Head of Data Solutions has regained his composure. "Of course, we have been very careful about the way that our systems have been developed. We have the very highest standards and have implemented the latest technologies to make sure the integrity of the data products is maintained, from acquisition, through packaging, to selection and transportation."

That'd be a no, then. You resist the urge to raise an eyebrow. That's another point you'll definitely be including in the report. No matter how slick your systems and processes, you've always got to allow your customers to provide feedback; but looking at the expression your guide is making, it's clear that there's no point in making the argument here. "OK, in that case, please could you show me how your 'strong automated quality control' works?"

There's an almost imperceptible wince before you get your reply: "Yes, I'd be delighted to show you. I'm sure you'll be impressed. It really is cutting edge."

You're taken down to one of the loading bays and the process for one of the deliveries is temporarily paused so that the Head of Data Solutions can talk you through the way it works. Unsurprisingly, everything is automated. Every data product is assigned a metadata barcode when it's acquired, and that barcode is used at every point through the data product's journey through the warehouse. It's the metadata contained within each barcode, that's used to enable the storage of the data products in the right places, and is used by the transport buggies to easily and accurately select the right data products for delivery to specific stores, when they place orders.

Reviewing the details, you've got to admit, you are pretty impressed. You can see that, in theory, it's fool-proof. The trouble is, you've seen the mess of mis-labelled products that have been making their way into the stores. You shake your head. The problem's got to be at the point the warehouse acquires the products. Something's got to be going wrong when they're tagged with barcodes, because the system from that point to here is clearly well designed. You decide not to embarrass your chaperon by opening up a box to see what's in there. There'll be time for that when you go to the data products staging area, where data products are acquired and brought into the warehouse.

The Head of Data Solutions already knows where you want to go next. You head back to the transport buggy and he punches in the commands.

## The Data Products Staging Area

A light drizzle has started to descend on the warehouse as you clamber out of the transport buggy at the Data Products Staging Area. This is where all of the data products get delivered into the warehouse from various suppliers and from other warehouses across the Data Country. The entrance to the staging area is the least impressive part of your tour so far, albeit seemingly even bigger than the rest of the facility. There's a vast, open-air car park, where a long line of lorries forms a queue, their contents removed by forklifts similar to those that you saw in the distribution port.

As before, the Head of Solutions applies a temporary pause to one of the lorries that is being unloaded so you can take a look at how the process is working.

You eagerly open the first box that you come to, but when you see the labels on the data products inside, your heart sinks. You're not looking at the names of the products, you're looking at the brightly coloured logo of the company that produces them. "Trusted Metadata Solutions." It's the last company that you provided consulting services to and the main reference that you used to get this job.

"Is everything OK?" There is a note of concern in the Head of Solution's voice.

If it turns out that Trusted Metadata Solutions' products are part of the problem, this could be a blow to your credibility. It was their reference that got you this job. You don't look up or respond; instead, you reach out for the first data product and open it. Then you stand back and look at the box.

Sure enough, it's as you feared: all three are mis-matches. The labels on the outer box, the titles on the inner packages and the data products themselves are all totally different. "Trusted Metadata Solutions", the organisation that you'd held up as a shining example of retail best practice, is one of the sources of the problems.

Oh well, there's nothing for it. You try to shake off a wave of anxiety, as you imagine the reaction to this revelation. You know you've got to do your job, even if it does mean highlighting the poor performance of the company you've previously proudly shared as a case study for retail processing excellence.

"I'm afraid I've found a problem," you say, looking up at the Head of

Solutions, who moves in to take a closer look. "The metadata descriptions on the outer box and the data product packaging don't match, and even worse than that, the data products themselves aren't what their product packaging says they are."

The Head of Solutions is surprisingly unperturbed. "Well, we can't be held accountable for our suppliers' mistake!"

"Unfortunately, you can," you reply, "because your customers don't care where in the supply chain things go wrong, they just care that they've gone wrong and will hold your company accountable. Given how widespread these problems are, it's putting your entire operation at risk."

"But our systems are fool-proof! They use the most advanced technology in the industry and are optimised for efficiency! We hit every single one of our throughput targets, every time!"

"I understand," you say patiently, "and I do agree that your systems are advanced, but I'm here to advise on what needs to be improved. I'm not here to cause trouble, I'm here to help."

"Well fine, but it's not our problem, it's our suppliers!" snaps the Head of Solutions, his confidence clearly waning.

"To a certain extent, you're right," you start, holding your hands up to calm him down, "so the key question then becomes: how do you identify when a supplier has put the wrong metadata on their packaging and how do you feed back to them? You should have clauses in the contracts that you signed with them, which holds them to certain standards, and should be able to return data products to them that don't meet those standards and also get some form of compensation from them for the impact of their mistakes."

"We can't check every box that comes through here! There are millions of data products processed every day! We'd never meet out throughput targets!"

"What about your quality targets?" The blank reaction to your question says it all. "Are you saying the only thing you're measured on is throughput?" you ask.

The Head of Solutions nods, looking numb.

"OK, well that needs to change. It seems to me that you're doing exactly as you're told, but you're being incentivised based on efficiency only, when it's the quality of what you're processing that's actually causing the majority of the problems for front-line stores and customers. I'm not saying that you need to check every box that comes through here, but you'll need to start doing sample checks of data products coming through from each of your suppliers and if you find problems you need to get them reported and you need to manage their performance. One other thing: what happens if you receive data products that don't have any metadata on them at all?"

The Head of Solutions blinks. "Oh, um, well they just get tagged as 'Miscellaneous' and get sent straight to the 'Misc' part of the warehouse."

You nod calmly. "OK, and how many items do you receive like that? Do you know which suppliers provide them?"

His head shakes, "I don't know, but quite a few, I think. It wouldn't be hard to find out."

"That's a pretty common problem, but that needs to be treated in the same way, OK? Missing metadata labels are just as bad as incorrect ones: they make it impossible for you to process them properly and cause all kinds of problems for the downstream supply chain."

Your guide regains some of his composure again and looks back at you. "What are you going to do now?"

You sigh. "Well, my next steps are the same as always: I'm going to write up a report with my findings and recommendations and present it to senior management. It's up to them to decide what to do next." You smile reassuringly, "Don't worry, I'll make sure I include the good things in my report, too. You'll be fine. My recommendations are all about making things better and I've delivered plenty of presentations like this in the past. It'll be fine."

With that, you're done. The Head of Solutions escorts you to the entrance and you head back towards your car, leaving the imposing architecture of the warehouse behind you. You know what you need to do next. You wonder how senior management will react, but that's for you to worry about tomorrow...

**Lesson 5:**

*Metadata management is like supply chain orchestration. You need to label and track your stock to be able to optimise logistics and meet customer expectations. Understanding what data you have and where it is, is crucial to delivering value from it.*

# 6. THE DATA LITERACY DRIVING SCHOOL

## The reluctant student

You look over at your driving instructor and sigh. *Why do I have to do this again?* you think. Taking data taxis had always been fine before. This seems like it's going to be a lot of effort, and for what?

Your company's enrolled you on a mandatory data literacy driving course. For years, data employees have been paying to use other people's data cars to get places, but after a series of wasted journeys and large-scale data car crashes, there has been a decision to educate everyone on how to drive. Someone realised that if people didn't know how to drive a data car, they wouldn't be able to effectively direct a data taxi driver to get the best out of their journey.

At this point, you're pretty sure you're never going to need to use these new skills that you're learning. Taxis have always got you to where you needed to go in the past. OK, so the costs can add up, but they work, as long as you give them clear instructions.

Your cheeks flush as you remember that embarrassing time a taxi driver took you on a two-hour detour, charging you twice as much as the journey was worth, and you didn't even realise. That's why you were so high up the list of people to be trained. Ever since then, you'd been forced to stick to buses, until you'd obtained your data literacy driving license and shown that you know how to drive key work routes. Buses are slow and makes lots of stops, but they're cheap and get you from A to B, so you're far less likely to get scammed or be involved in an accident, even if they do take longer.

OK, it's got to be done. Let's get on with this… You turn your head and smile nervously, as your instructor starts to talk you through the various alien-looking dials and instruments in front of you. As you sit there, brow furrowed as you try to grasp the new terms and instructions that you're being bombarded with, it does make you pause to think: *how is it that I've been driven around all my life and didn't come to know any of this before? There's so much to get my head around, do all taxi drivers really know all this stuff? Does it really take this much to do something as simple as driving down the road?…*

## Discovering The Unknown Unknowns

The first thing your instructor talks you through is an overview of how everything works. To your relief, he doesn't just ask you to start the engine straight away. He explains what things are, how they work, and key things to look out for when you get started. His explanations provide you with the framework of terminology that enable you to understand what he's talking about when you get on the road and he's instructing you on where to go.

There are a set of dials that are used to monitor how the car's operating. The key ones tell you how much data fuel is in the tank, how many data revolutions the engine is making and what the car's current data quality speed is. You learn that you need to keep checking these dials to monitor the performance of the car and to make sure you're running it properly. You need to know if you're about to run out of fuel; if the revs are too high or too low; and you need to keep an eye on the data speed so you don't go too fast or too slow.

Next, you're introduced to the data driving controls. The steering wheel enables you to direct the data car, pointing it down different data roads and up the insight alleys that you want to explore. Your data gear stick gives you control over the direction of the car and the gears in the engine, taking you up and down aggregation levels as your speed changes; and there are pedals that you use in combination with the gear stick to speed up or slow down. You also need to keep checking your mirrors to make sure you see other data cars to avoid collisions. The majority of data accidents are caused by other data cars with their own problems, which crash into other data cars that were absolutely fine before, scratching them up or bashing holes in them.

There are so many things to remember, and you've not even started the engine yet. Suddenly you have a newfound appreciation for the data taxi drivers. They may just provide a commodity service, but you're also starting to see why understanding all these things might help you, even if you are just sat watching someone else drive. You're going to be able to tell if they're doing a good job or not. Are they checking their mirrors to keep you safe? Are they using their gears properly to run the car economically and get you places as efficiently as possible?

"Right," says the instructor, "I think it's time to give it a go for real. Make sure you're in neutral and start the engine, just as I described, please."

You take a breath and turn the ignition. The engine rumbles into life. Here we go…

## The awkward first drive

It's relatively easy for you to get the car to move forwards, although it feels a bit awkward at first. The car shudders and stutters a bit as your unsteady feet control the pedals, but fairly soon you find yourself moving cautiously forwards, eyes darting between the road and the mirrors, suddenly conscious of how much you need to be aware of as you navigate from the driving school's car park towards the main road.

The instructor tells you to stop the data car at the entrance of the data driving school, before you get onto the road. You both sit in silence for a moment, surveying the scene before you. The driving school is on the top of a hill, which provides a clear line of sight over the sprawling spaghetti of roads and buildings that makes up Transaction Data City. You can see the mass of traffic clogging the streets below and, in the distance, can see the fast-moving cars that are speeding across town on the data highway. You can't help but gasp, knowing that you're going to be entering into this complex metropolis, responsible for getting through the packed streets to an as yet unknown destination.

"Something you need to know about data driving," the instructor announces, breaking the silence, "is that it's not just about moving, or getting to some random location."

He shifts his weight in his seat and turns to look at you. "You see, it's really important that you know where you're trying to get to and how to get there in the most sensible way. This city is a very dangerous place. There are many routes that you can take, which will lead you to the same destination; but some are far slower than others, and some have unseen pitfalls that many a data driver has fallen down, never to be seen again."

As if on cue, a dull explosion can be heard in the distance. A knowing smile spreads across the instructor's face. "Ah. A great example of the kind of data dead-end that you don't want to go down. Lots of time wasted and it'll inevitably lead to bad decisions and bad outcomes for you and the data people you're driving."

You turn to look back at the urban labyrinth before you. "I thought this lesson was just about how to drive the car," you exclaim.

"Well, that will get you so far," chuckles the instructor, "but your company is paying for you to learn how to get somewhere useful, and ideally in one piece, not just to be able to drive around aimlessly, wasting their time and money. There's got to be a point to your data journeys, because otherwise why are you travelling at all?"

You nod, understanding, but also realising that there's even more to this than you'd bargained for.

"OK," the instructor says as he nods towards a tall building in the distance. "We're heading for your company's HQ. It's across town, so we're not going to use the back roads because it'll take too long. We need to head to the data highway. Do your checks and you can start when you're ready."

So you start to move again, shakily steering down the street, clunkily shifting gears and making slow progress towards your destination.

Your data instructor directs you at every turn, so you can focus on using the data car's controls properly. You find that everything you're doing requires thought and effort, as you mind gets used to the range of actions that you need to take to control and steer the data car.

Before long, you've reached your company's headquarters and your first lesson is over. Your instructor guides you through a review on how your first drive went. "Every time you drive your data car, take the time to think about your journey. What went well and what didn't? Did you choose the right route? Is there anything you'd do differently, next time? No matter how many times you drive, you can always learn and be a better driver. It's keeping an open, learning mindset that will lead you to consistently successful journeys. Don't ever become complacent. You never know what unexpected data car crash is around the corner, which will take you by surprise and force you to adapt. Stay alert, keep learning, and you'll be ready to drive on your own in no time…"

## Avoiding dead-ends

As time goes by, you find yourself increasingly confident in your driving. The data car seems to move more smoothly as you manipulate the controls with increasing aptitude. You find yourself able to concentrate better, without your attention flitting between all the various things you need to remember, and you're using the dials as though you've always known how to use them.

It's still taking quite a bit of effort to remember everything you need to do and there's the odd time that you crunch the gears or swerve a bit too close to the curb, but the instructor is able to sit back and say less and less as you show you know what you're doing.

*How on earth did I get by before?* you think, as you drive along, remembering how clueless and helpless you'd been when you were just a passenger in a taxi, totally dependent on your driver to take you wherever you needed to go. You remember how many people you've known, who have been taken to completely the wrong destination, simply because they had no idea what they were signing up for.

It's at this point that the driving instructor starts to talk again; but this time, not just about where you're going, but also pointing out other data archive alleys and data insight dead-ends to avoid. When he starts pointing them out, you suddenly become aware of just how many there are and how easy it would be to go down some of them. To the untrained eye, they could look just like some of the other roads you've been driving down, but some lead to the wrong destination. There's one analytical short-cut that your instructor points out, where it takes half the time and leads to somewhere that looks like the right place, but many a data person has lost their life when they actually tried to get out there. Then there are the routes that take many times longer to get to the same place. If you don't know what you're doing, you could easily go down them and might not even know you've taken a wrong turn until it's too late and you're committed to a lengthy detour.

"You can learn a lot from other data drivers", the instructor says, "and as long as you're learning from someone who's experienced and done the journey a few times before, that's a good thing to do, because it'll save you a lot of time." As he's talking, he points to a road that he wants you to turn down and you follow his direction. "However, the only way to become really good at data navigation is by doing it yourself. That could be navigating for someone else who's driving, or planning a route that you drive yourself, but you need to understand the roads and how to plot a course, which means you can't learn by just getting other people to do it without taking any interest in the journey."

You nod in agreement. It hasn't taken long to realise how important what you're learning is. By having to drive the data car yourself, you can now see why knowledge on its own isn't enough: real experience is crucial for being able to safely get to your destination.

## Missing signs and potholes

Your next set of lessons is about dangers on the road and how to avoid them.

The first one surprises you: it's about road signs. As you're driving down a road that your instructor has taken you several times before, he asks you to look up and see if there's anything that you can see that's missing. You shake your head: it all looks the same as it's always looked, to you.

"OK," the instructor responds, "so if you'd never been down this road before, how would you know where you are?"

Then it hits you. There are no road signs, at all. Nothing to say what road you're on, what the speed limit is, or anything. Then you notice there aren't even any road markings. You're astounded that you've never noticed it before.

The instructor chuckles at your reaction. "Never go down a data road without any metadata signs up, unless you're with someone that really knows the area, because otherwise you're going to get yourself lost. Transaction Data City is full of roads like this. The builders just didn't bother putting any signs up, because they thought people would just know where they're going. I guess, when this was just a small town, it didn't matter so much, but now there are big areas where data people can get complete lost. I've heard about data people going missing for days, as they go round and round in circles and then end up re-appearing where they went in, no closer to their destination but very tired and frustrated from their rather unproductive adventure."

"Why don't the government put up new signs, if it's such a problem?"

"Oh, yes, well there is a huge Meta-project to do just that, but once the builders have gone, it's ten times harder to work out what each road should be called and where it leads. That's why the project's costing so much and taking so much time: each road needs to be properly surveyed and experts need to be built in to make sure the signs are right. There were past attempts

71

to do this on the cheap, but it resulted in the wrong metadata signs being put up and people ended up going completely the wrong way: it was even worse than having no signs at all!"

You shake your head. Surely it's obvious that signs should be put up when the road's built; but then, it can't be that obvious, if there are so many roads like this.

Your instructor asks you to go down a side road, to show you another common challenge. You find out what it is straight away: there's a violent BANG as one of your wheels bounces over a pothole. You gasp and clamber to regain control.

"Careful," your instructor advises, "you need to go slower down this road. There are lots of holes, where big chunks of the road are missing. It's dangerous and can result in damage to your data car."

"This is crazy," you exclaim. "How's anyone expected to drive down a road that has so many problems?"

"Well, there are some roads that you can't drive down at all, as it turns out. They're in such a bad state, they're totally unusable. And yet, that doesn't stop people trying to use them. It's surprising, really, when it's quite easy to see how poor the quality of the data road is, why people think they can still use it. Park at the side of the road over there for a moment, please."

You do as you're told and turn to hear what your instructor has to say next.


**Being a responsible data driver**

"Now," your driving instructor continues, "you've come a long way since your first lesson. You can comfortably control a data car and have shown that you are developing good navigational skills. You also now understand some of the pitfalls that can result in you going down the wrong data insight alley or that can completely prevent you from progressing. There is one last, important lesson, which I've brought you to this sorry road to explain."

You're a bit taken aback by your instructor's kind words. You know that you've been making good progress, but didn't realise you were so close to being ready to get your license. "Thanks, that's great to hear. What is your final lesson?"

"This final lesson is something that even many experienced data drivers never seem to grasp; and yet, it's so important for everyone on the road, if we all want to be able to go on many successful data journeys across this great and complex city of ours. The thing is, if you are a data driver, you are a user of these data roads, and it's in your best interest for the data roads to be in good condition." He nods towards the poor quality of the road surface in front of you. Turning to look at you again, he continues: "If you find problems with quality of the data road surface, you need to report it to the Data Quality Council. You're just a data driver, so you can't fix any of these potholes yourself, but if you also don't notify the council, they won't know about the problems and won't be able to fix them."

"But don't the council have their own people, who go out and find and fix problems with the roads?"

"Yes, they do," your instructor confirms, "but the city's so big, they don't have enough people to keep an eye on everything that's going on, so could easily miss some really major data road quality problems, unless responsible data drivers report them. By using the data roads, you need to become a steward of the data roads, yourself. If you, and all other data drivers, don't take responsibility and don't play their part, then you can't complain when you find the roads are unusable and you can't get places."

"OK," you nod, "that makes sense. How do I report a data road problem to the council?"

"Fortunately, it's quite easy nowadays. A few years back, they realised that part of the reason no-one was reporting anything to them was because they hadn't made it clear how to do it. There's a website and an app that you can use, and the council are starting to put signs up that give a few other options, too."

## Driving to work

Two weeks after that final lesson, you pass your test and get your data literacy driving license. You're provided with a company data car to drive and even offer some of your ex-colleagues lifts.

Within weeks, you're driving all over the place. You're running deliveries, helping senior management get places they've never been before, and haven't had a single data car crash or wasted data journey.

You're so productive, you get a promotion. Who would've thought that knowing how to drive a data car could make you so much more valuable to your company?

Congratulations! You're now the Head of Data Driving Stewards.

---

**Lesson 6:**

*Data Literacy is like knowing how to drive. Mis-using data can result in a data car crash, so the better educated people are in how to understand and use data, the more value they will be able to deliver with it, in faster, more effective and safer ways.*

---

# CONCLUSION: A NEW WAY OF THINKING

**"Stories are up to 22 times more memorable than facts."**
*Jennifer Aaker, Social Psychologist, Professor at Stanford Graduate School of Business*

## Bringing it all together

If there's one thing I'd like you to take away from reading this book, it's how important data literacy is, for everyone in your organisation. This collection of stories provides a foundation for data literacy and I hope they open people's eyes to the significance and value of the topics they cover.

As **The Data Literacy Driving School** showed, a lack of data literacy can result in a "data car crash", whereas a good level of data literacy can lead to outstanding results.

When you compare data management to real-world scenarios, it quickly becomes apparent how essential certain activities are, along with the potentially catastrophic impact of not doing them properly.

Whilst the data cars falling off the "sticky plaster flyover" in **The Data Architecture Construction Project** may be funny to imagine, the reality is, poorly designed and implemented data architecture really can result in data going completely missing!

Likewise, if you don't maintain your metadata, it is quite literally the same as not labelling products in a retail supply chain and will cause similarly disastrous outcomes to those that occurred in **The Metadata Mess**. A lack of good quality metadata is an extremely common cause of issues on even the smallest of data projects (even if the term "metadata" isn't always used).

Every one of these stories provides insights into the data management practices that will make the difference between success and failure. Data management is a never-ending task, as explained in **The Data Garden**. It is essential to establish data governance, as outlined in **The Data Governance Country**, and there are real similarities between managing data quality in a business and managing **The Data Quality Hospital**.

The other thing that is important to note is the overlap and inter-dependencies between these stories. Although there are a number of discrete data management disciplines covered here, all of these practices are needed together to deliver success.

For example, if you focus on data quality on its own but never fix the underlying data architecture that your data flows through, you're going to be fighting a never-ending battle against the same data problems. It's like working on a garden that keeps flooding, but instead of fixing the drainage you just keep buying more buckets.

**Get data gardening!**

I hope you found this book interesting, thought provoking and fun to read.

The key now is for you to take these lessons and put them into action, so you can drive value through the effective management and use of the data in your organisation!

Which of the approaches and techniques can you apply in your company now? Are there things that aren't getting enough attention because they're misunderstood? Are there people who you could now better explain these concepts to, so you can gain their support and drive action?

Whatever you do next, you should now have a better understanding of data management than you had before, from a number of new perspectives, which will help you be far more effective when working on any data transformation initiative.

I've enjoyed sharing these little stories with you and wish you well in your Data journey, whether you're an executive sponsoring a data initiative, an aspiring Chief Data Gardening Officer or someone who's taking on some other exciting Data role. Good luck!

# APPENDIX:
# THE 6 KEY DATA MANAGEMENT LESSONS

**Lesson 1:**
*Data Management is like gardening. It's a never-ending task, because data keeps growing in volume and variety; but with the right expertise and leadership, and by utilising the right techniques and tools, you can keep your data well maintained, and cultivate it to deliver outstanding value.*

**Lesson 2:**
*Data Governance is like running a country. It's crucial to successfully steer a wide range of inter-connected activities that involve a lot of people, and requires experienced leadership, clear communication and coordination, to optimise the value delivered using finite resources.*

**Lesson 3:**
*Data Quality Management is like running a hospital. Data needs to be healthy (its data quality needs to be maintained), for it to be used for its intended purpose. It's important to implement a dynamic process for diagnosing, prioritising and treating data issues, based on their severity and business value.*

**Lesson 4:**
*Data Architecture is like delivering a large infrastructure building project. Connecting good design theory to practical delivery, and coordinating the efforts of multiple delivery and maintenance teams, can make the difference between a costly mess and amazing success.*

**Lesson 5:**
*Metadata management is like supply chain orchestration. You need to label and track your stock to be able to optimise logistics and meet customer expectations. Understanding what data you have and where it is, is crucial to delivering value from it.*

**Lesson 6:**
*Data Literacy is like knowing how to drive. Mis-using data can result in a data car crash, so the better educated people are in how to understand and use data, the more value they will be able to deliver with it, in faster, more effective and safer ways.*

# ACKNOWLEDGMENTS

I've been honoured by the positive support I've received in the development of this book and have many people I'd like to thank.

Of course I must start with my wife Michelle for all her love and support: she does so much for me and our children and I am blessed to have her in my life. She also helped with the design of the book cover!
*Thank you for everything, my love!*

Also for my children Tristan, Elysia and Ethan, whose sense of fun, curiosity and joy are an inspiration.
*I am more proud of you than you could imagine!*

I'd like to say a massive thank you to my parents, Mick and Jill, who were the first people to review the early drafts of this book and were with me throughout the writing journey, providing both support and constructive feedback to make it better.
*Thank you for your help with this book and for always being such an amazing support in everything I do!*

I also want to say thank you to Michelle's parents, Jeremy and Romaine.
*You've always made me feel very welcome as your son-in-law and I appreciate all you've done for us as a family!*

Next I've got to say a big thank-you to David Blackwell, who has been a great friend and supporter over many years and was the first person outside of my family to read a draft of this book.
*As always, your advice was excellent – especially the idea to add in the "lessons", which give the stories a more practical "kicker". Thank you!*

Thanks must also go to Victoria Ball, for generously taking the time to review the stories and provide positive feedback and ideas.
*Your input as a business professional and non-data-expert really helped and was much appreciated!*

At the time of writing, I am working as Data Protection Officer for Nationwide Building Society in the UK and I want to say thanks to all the great people that I have the privilege to work with and call my colleagues.

In particular, I'd like to thank Joe Garner, CEO, who was very supportive when I contacted him about this book.

I'd also like to thank Simone Steele, CDO, for her support and for her insightful feedback on the book.

Next I'd like to say a big thanks to Matt Smith, Deputy DPO, for being such a great and dependable colleague and friend, and for his feedback on the ideas in these allegories.

*Thank you for your commitment and humour, and in particular your passion for records management, which was the inspiration for the "living dead" part of the Data Governance Country. (I'm glad you liked it!)*

There are a few other people who I'd like to say a special thanks to, for agreeing to review this book before it was published; for their ideas and support; and for the positive impact they have had not only on this book but also on my career and professional life over the years. For these things, I'd like to say a massive thank-you to (in alphabetical order):

Gareth Davies
Nigel Walder
Rob McKendrick
Rodney Coutinho
Simon Driscoll
Simon Williams

I'd also like to thank my editor, Claire Rushbrook, for her professional, clear and efficient help on this book.

Finally, I'd like to give a shout-out to the Alpha Group that I joined during the Covid-19 lockdown (which happened to coincide with the writing of this book). They are the nicest group of people I could have hoped to meet and it's been great getting to know them: Courtney & Jeff, Funmi, Jamie, Jemma, Jenny, Lamidé, Maureen, Michael, Niel, Tiffany and Victoria.

Thank you everyone – you've all made a massive difference and I'm very grateful.

# ABOUT THE AUTHOR

Paul Jones is an expert in large-scale, enterprise-wide data transformation delivery and is an evangelist about the value of effective data management.

He advises Boards and CxO-level stakeholders on how to realise the strategic value of data and how to translate theory into practical outcomes.

Paul is passionate about mentoring and coaching people to succeed and gets great pleasure in sharing his knowledge and helping others...

...and after this book, I guess you could call him a "data storyteller" too!

Paul is married with three children and lives in Hampshire, England.

http://www.pauldanieljones.com

http://www.linkedin.com/in/pauldanieljonesuk/